JUST MY TYPO

COMPILED BY DRUMMOND MOIR

SCEPTRE

Picture Acknowledgements
© Matthew McDermott/Polaris/eyevine: 125. © Press Association Images:
40 photo Byron Rollins, 46 photo Susan Walsh, 82 photo Aliosha Marquez.
© Brendan Smialowski/AFP/Getty Images: 45.

First published in Great Britain in 2012 by Sceptre
An imprint of Hodder & Stoughton
An Hachette UK company

1

Copyright © Drummond Moir 2012

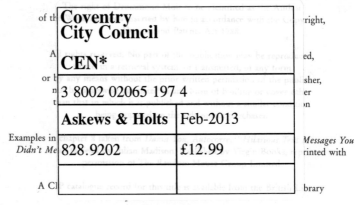

Hardback ISBN 978 1 444 75997 6
Ebook ISBN 978 1 444 75998 3

Typeset in Stempel Garamond by
Palimpsest Book Production Limited, Falkirk, Stirlingshire

Printed and bound by Clays Ltd, St Ives plc

Hodder & Stoughton Ltd
338 Euston Road
London NW1 3BH

www.sceptrebooks.co.uk

The Coventry City Council library stamp overlaid on the page reads:

Coventry City Council CEN*	
3 8002 02065 197 4	
Askews & Holts	Feb-2013
828.9202	£12.99

'A book may be amusing with numerous errors, or it may be very dull without a single absurdity.'

Publisher's advertisement for Oliver Goldsmith's 1766 novel *The Vicar of Wakefield*

'Every time you make a typo, the errorists win.'

Facebook slogan

Contents

Note to the reader

All typos in this book are intentional.

Any typos made by the compiling editor are also intentional, and are there purely for comic effect.

If during the course of reading this book you think you spot a typo, you haven't. If you think you might have spotted one all the same, you haven't.

No typos will be corrected for future editions.

Editor's Introduction

During work experience at one of London's most prestigious publishing houses, my first task was to check the uncorrected proofs of a thousand-page biography of Kingsley Amis. Full of zeal and armed with my degree in English Language and Literature, I'd resolved to keep a list of any word I came across that I didn't know, in order to become as literate, and literary, as possible.

Somewhere around page 600 I came across 'oppobrium'. What, I wondered, could this mean? Trembling with excitement at the idea of expanding my modest vocabulary, I reached for my trusty *Oxford English Dictionary*.

Only 'oppobrium' isn't a word. 'Opprobrium' is a word, but 'oppobrium' manifestly is not. I checked it, checked it again, and resolved to mark it up in blue pen (which denotes a publisher's, rather than typesetter's, error), trying (but failing) to use the correct proofreading symbol. When asked the next morning how I was getting on, I replied casually that I'd finished the book, and loved it. But, I hope they didn't mind, I spotted a typo.

You caught a typo while speed-reading a thousand-page tome? In the midst of 300,000 words about one of the geniuses of English letters, you picked up a missing 'r' in a cumbersome, awkward, skim-it-it's-too-clever-for-mere-mortals word? They looked at me like I was Rain Man. I was offered a job shortly after, and at the back of my mind this entirely fluky observation (the result of ignorance, of course, rather than wisdom) is what made all the difference.

Having worked in publishing for a few years, though, I now realise this is nonsense. How wise I felt, spotting that typo, but how utterly banal it must have seemed. There are typos everywhere: in legal documents, medical reports, Bibles, NASA calculations and government papers. Typos have caused immense embarrassment and obscenity, provoked lawsuits, scuppered careers, caused offence, costs millions of pounds, dollars and pesos, shamed paragons of virtue and – I don't have an example, but I bet it's true – ended marriages.

Because we all make mistakes. No matter which field of human endeavour, regardless of how meticulous we are, how many times we check, what systems we have in place to catch the inevitable howler: every now and then we make a mistake. I know this from painful, painful experience. Show me a typo in a book I've edited or published, a blurb I've sent to an author, a letter I've painstakingly composed or a note I've scrawled to remind me to do something, and I will feel like you've taken my first-born. I will be heartbroken, crestfallen, consumed with self-pity and utterly, utterly furious. Because there is nothing more crushing, more bruising, more humiliating, more mortifying or more upsetting – to an editor, at least – than a typo.

Thankfully though (deep breath), it's usually not life or death. When soldiers, doctors, politicians, bomb disposal squads and hostage negotiators make mistakes, people actually die. (Though typos in these realms can also be rather dangerous – imagine, if you will, a letter from your doctor asking you to exorcise rather than exercise, recommending that you rust rather than rest, or imploring you to die rather than diet.) When authors, publishers, journalists and other esteemed members of the literati strive to write flawless, orthographically perfect prose it can often feel like the most important thing in the world . . .

But let's face it, it probably isn't.

So here is a selection of typos which, like any typo of any kind, should never have happened, cannot be excused, and must not in any way be glorified. But they happened, so we might as well enjoy them.[1]

Reliability
...always upholding the highest standards for every detal.

Marketing slogan for a greeting card company. You couldn't make it up . . .

---

1 I've tried my utmost to limit examples and anecdotes to instances where a single letter, punctuation mark or space is in the wrong place at the wrong time. The occasional exception has been made, however, to accommodate a few howlers that were just too funny to omit.

To Be or To Be

Typos in Literature

The title of this chapter, 'To be or to be', a bastardisation of one of the most famous sentences in the English language, comes from a new edition of Shakespeare's *Hamlet* published some years ago. Six professional proofreaders failed to catch the mistake, which received national publicity.

'I am certain of one thing. Whatever may come between us – and wherever he may be on earth – Arthur will always remember that I love ham.'

The Parting, Millicent Hemming

My love she's handsome, my love she's boney.

A Portrait of the Artist as a Young Man, James Joyce

'Barney', by Rudge – $1.50

New York publisher's advertisement for Charles Dickens' fifth novel, late nineteenth century

After being moved to tears by the sheer scale of CERN's particle accelerator, the Large Hadron Collider, Richard Dawkins attempted to express his awe in his new book. But in what he described as 'an unfortunate misprint', the object of his affection came out as 'The Large Hardon Collider'.

MY FAVOURITE TYPO

Catriona McPherson, novelist

'I once found the following typo while editing one of my Dandy Gilver mysteries. The context is that Dandy (a respectable, gently born sleuth from the 1920s) hears the door of an adjacent room slam. I meant to have "I opened my own a crack and put my eye to it" . . . only I'd missed out the word "a". I'm ashamed to tell you how long I laughed for.'

He was disfigured. As long as I can remember, he has had a car on his face.

Short story

Ted could not raise the cash necessary to purchase a house, and eventually in desperation he had to burrow.

The Price of Love, Rosemary Jeans

The poet Alfred Noyes (1880–1958) once wrote a lovely elegy for a soldier who lay dead in a distant war. The poem depicted a family dreaming of the homecoming of their soldier, while 'All night he lies beneath the stars / And dreams no more out there.' When the *Irish Times* printed the poem, it became 'All night he lies beneath the stairs . . .'

He could see hills on the horizon. The hills were dark yellow and black. Past the hills, he guessed, was the dessert.

2666, Roberto Bolaño

He stiffened for a moment but then she felt his muscles loosen as he shitted on the ground.

Baby, I'm Yours, Susan Andersen

The doctor smiled reassuringly at the worried mother and patted her little bot on the cheek.

Prescription for Love, Josephine Lawrence

MY FAVOURITE TYPO

Erica Wagner, Literary Editor, The Times, *London*

'When I first came to *The Times*, sixteen years ago (!), our reviewers would post in their copy, or, if they were really technologically advanced, fax it. I would then write a catchline on top of the piece, and put it in a tray to go down to the copytakers, who would swiftly and efficiently type it into our creaky Atex system. Peter Ackroyd reviewed a biography of George Bernard Shaw for me in those olden days, in which he referred to GBS as 'the man in the Jaeger suit'. It came back from the copytakers as 'the man in the jaguar suit' – an image of GBS I have always loved . . .'

> **Later that same evening after a vain search all around the village, Mary found the dog dead in the garden. She curried the body indoors.**
>
> *Life in Barnsthorpe*, Patricia Cox

Towards the end of Herman Melville's 1850 novel *White Jacket*, an account of a sailor's fall into the sea includes the following passage: 'But of a sudden some fashion-less form brushed my side – some inert, coiled fish of the sea'. In the early 1920s, when the Standard Edition of Melville's works was first published in London, a typesetter hit the wrong key and 'coiled fish' became 'soiled fish'. Two decades later, a noted Harvard literary critic (who I'm not going to name) analysed the passage in a published work about the golden era of American literature. Unaware that 'soiled' was a misprint, he praised the passage as 'a twist of imagery of the sort that would become peculiarly Melville's,' going on to assert, rather gushingly, that 'hardly anyone but Melville could have created the shudder that results from calling this frightening vagueness some "soiled fish of the sea".'

> **Harry detached himself from the body and stepped across the concrete floor to a bunker door he had noticed. With his lighter lit he was a target; with more light everyone was a target. He held the MP5 at the ready while fucking the switch with his left hand.**
>
> Unedited draft of Jo Nesbø's *Phantom*

POETS' CORNER

Typos in literature are nothing new. Geoffrey Chaucer was so enraged by one of his fourteenth-century scribes, Adam Pinkhurst, that he wrote a poem to name and shame him. The verse ends:

So oft a day I must thy work renew,
It to correct, and eke to rub and scrape;
And all is through thy negligence and rape.

Others too have suffered at the pen of an irate poet. In the early nineteenth century, Irishman Thomas Moore composed the following lines about the incompetence of English printers:

But 'tis dreadful to think what provoking mistakes
The vile country press in one's prosody makes.
For you know, dear, – I may, without vanity, hint –
Though an angel should write, still 'tis devils must print;
And you can't think what havoc these demons sometimes
Choose to make of one's sense, and, what's worse, of one's rhymes.

But a week or two since, in my Ode upon Spring,
Which I meant to have made a most beautiful thing,
Where I talk'd of the 'dewdrops from freshly-blown roses,'
The nasty things made it 'from freshly blown noses'!
                                        The Fudges in England, 1835

From his left ear to the corner of his mouth ran a long scar, the result of a duet many years before.

Flight From Germany, William le Queux

Page 140. In line 10 of 'Night Arrival of Sea-Trout', for 'rape', read 'nape'.

Erratum slip from Ted Hughes' 1979 collection *Moortown*

MY FAVOURITE TYPO

Alan Titchmarsh

'When employed as a gardening books editor some years ago, I was proofreading an entry in a gardening encyclopedia for pulmonaria, the lungwort, whose leaves are attractively spotted with white. It was only by sheer good fortune that I noticed the entry read:

Pulmonaria, the lungwort, whose leaves are attractively spotted with shite.'

---

5 Sept 2002 – In a report of the commemoration of Wordsworth's poem 'Composed Upon Westminster Bridge', page 12, yesterday, we insinuated a Guardian apostrophe so that the view from the bridge became, 'A sight so touching in it's majesty'.

Guardian Corrections and Clarifications

14 Sept 2002 – A correction, page 25, September 5, was contentious. It corrected the punctuation in a line from Wordsworth's poem 'Westminster Bridge', which had appeared in a report in the Guardian the previous day as: 'A sight so touching in it's majesty'. In fact the punctuation follows the 1807 edition and the apostrophe has been retained in all anniversary editions.

Guardian Corrections and Clarifications

MY FAVOURITE TYPO

Nigel Wilcockson, Publisher

'My two favourites are the fifties recipe book that included the following instruction about soufflés: "Try to avoid peeing in to the oven, as this will impair the flavor"; and the unfortunate fairy-tale book that had a series of running heads reading "The Four Fairy Queers".'

When eminent British publisher Secker & Warburg merged with The Harvill Press in 2005, the trade announcement featured a long list of illustrious writers who'd been published down the decades by two of the great London literary lists, including George Orwell, Umberto Eco, Boris Pasternak, and one 'Frank Kafka'.

MY FAVOURITE TYPO

Andrew Steeds, Simply Put Communication Consultancy

'One major publisher I've worked with once gave me a wonderful example of the dangers of global search and replace. An author, having submitted his Young Adult novel, decided at the last minute that he wanted to change the name of the protagonist from David to Sam (I think his wife had just given birth to their first son, whose name this was). No problem, said the publishers, we'll do a search and replace: we can manage it, even if it's near final proof stage.

What they failed to remember was that the protagonist was an A-level student, studying History of Art, who travels to Florence with his school as part of his course. Cue brilliant moment when he and his group sit in rapt wonder staring up at Michelangelo's glorious sculpture . . .'

2 Nov 1999 – In wishing the actor Juliet Stevenson happy 43rd birthday on Saturday, page 24, October 30, we listed among her hits *The Duchess of Mali*. This was inadvertent discrimination against John Webster's *Duchess of Malfi*.

Guardian Corrections and Clarifications

MY FAVOURITE TYPO

Judith Flanders, author & journalist

'Once, at Penguin, I passed a cover proof (yup, shame on me, I passed it) for Alexandre Dumas' *The Count of Monte Carlo* (well, everything *was* spelt correctly!).'

Joyce's 1922 *Ulysses* is one of the most ambitious, influential and notoriously difficult novels ever written. From an editorial point of view it is also one of the most fascinating, since the original was riddled with hundreds of errors necessitating numerous new editions, all seeking to be the definitive version. The late Dr Jack Dalton, a Joycean scholar, shocked devotees in 1961 by pointing out that some of the mistakes in the original *Ulysses* were plain old typos. 'Bread', for example, is printed as 'beard' in the 1922 text. Because the 265,000-word stream of consciousness novel was so challenging, leaving most readers baffled by its experimental prose, the errors went largely unnoticed, or at least unremarked, for forty years after publication. Joyce himself simply didn't have time to correct every single error he found in the first proofs, complaining in a letter just three months before publication: 'Working as I do amid piles of notes at a table in a hotel, I cannot possibly do this mechanical part with my wretched eye and a half.'

MY FAVOURITE TYPO

Anonymous publisher

'The worst one that's ever happened on my watch was on a book blurb:

". . . and goes on to paint a picture of the north as it is today and has always been: a setting of wild coastline, lakes and green dales inhabited by indominantly inventive north-erners, proud of their past and forging a future of brilliant new enterprises."

I've no idea how many times we checked this before the finished book came in and we realised "indominantly" just isn't a word.'

Plot is important, but the manner of preventing it is still more important.

Writers' Magazine

INTERLUDE

The Perils of the Oxycretin!

While *oxymorons* are figures of speech in which contradictory terms combine in a single phrase (living dead, open secret, same difference, old news etc.), *oxycretins* are two opposite words which can be housed within the same word. By removing a single letter, the whole word switches to the opposite meaning – the typographical equivalent to striding obliviously towards an undetonated bomb. The slightest slip of the pen can make all the difference:

One survived

None survived

*

Don't be absurd, my mother-in-law is entirely harmless

Don't be absurd, my mother-in-law is entirely charmless

*

Is there anything more lovely than the

laughter of children?

Is there anything more lovely than the

slaughter of children?

*

INTERLUDE

Covert offensive: the last thing our enemy
will be expecting!

Overt offensive: the last thing our enemy
will be expecting!

*

The newly crowned Queen declared immediately
that she would reign in style

The newly crowned Queen declared immediately
that she would resign in style

Lastly, witness the following correction printed in the *Guardian*:

Owing to a typographical error Thursday's
article referred to the Soviet formula which
recognised the 'futility' of nuclear war. This
should have read 'utility'.

2

The Fourth Mistake

Typos in the Media

The Victorian newspaper the *London Globe* once made the following correction: 'Our printer yesterday committed a serious error in giving our extract from the registrar-general's return. He makes us say that the inhabitants of London suffer at present from a high rate of morality.'

THE QUEEN HERSELF GRACIOUSLY PISSED OVER THE MAGNIFICENT EDIFICE

The Times reporting Queen Victoria's opening of the Menai Bridge

MY FAVOURITE TYPO

Simon Heffer, journalist and author of Strictly English

'I seem to recall that when Violet, the mother of the Kray twins, died and they were let out for the day to attend her funeral, one newspaper described her obsequies as being those of "Mrs Violent Kray".'

Successful businesswoman, widower, aged 44,
usual trappings, non-smoker with varied inter-
ests, seeks affectionate, understanding female
to shave the enjoyable things in life.

Yorkshire Post

Timeless headline from the New Orleans
Times-Picayune, *2011*

BISHOPS AGREE SEX
ABUSE RULES

Sunday Business Post

WHEN TYPESETTERS LOSE IT
– NO. 53

On the other hand, Miss Wethered played
steadolly bm bm bm bm bm.

New York Morning Telegraph

'They have been suggesting that for some time. It's all rubbish. It's fiction.' His comments followed claims that the Prince has been secretly Mrs Parker-Bowles for more than a decade, and as often as once a week.

Evening Gazette

ONE CAN ARGUE THAT THE PRESIDENT IS USING THE SEPTEMBER 11 ATTACKS TO BOOST HIS PUBIC PROFILE

Christian Science Monitor on George Bush

And a Nightingale Sang (ITV) was like a stretched Hovis ad with some real acting. Set in Newcastle during the war, it had a bravura performance by Phyllis Logan as Helen, a lovely innocent lass who falls for squaddie (Tom Watt) whose compassionate manner conceals a belief that love is ultimately just a passing fanny.

Observer

During Woodrow Wilson's presidency, the *Washington Post* was credited with the 'most famous newspaper typo' in DC history. The *Post* intended to report that President Wilson had been 'entertaining' his future wife, Mrs Galt, but instead wrote that he had been 'entering' her.

MY FAVOURITE TYPO

Boyd Tonkin, Literary Editor, Independent

'Where do I start? Maybe with the distinguished chamber musician I once described as a rectal specialist . . . ?'

OLDER ADULTS:
You're sick. If you feel cold, put on a sweater, crap yourself in a blanket or turn up the heat, recommend the physicians.

> Public health announcement reported in the
> *Huffington Post*

ONE MAN WAS ADMITTED TO HOSPITAL SUFFERING FROM BUNS

Bristol Gazette

Last time out the Armagh boys accounted for Castleblaynet and the wide open spaces of Armagh will suit their style of play. It promises toben aeentr fuck it – to be an entertaining game, which could go either way.

Irish News

GERMANS ARE SO SMALL THAT THERE MAY BE AS MANY AS ONE BILLION, SEVEN HUNDRED MILLION OF THEM IN A DROP OF WATER

Mobile Press (US)

MY FAVOURITE TYPO

Alastair Campbell

'One of my most retweeted tweets was one where I had a hashtag #woefuk instead of #woeful . . . can't remember what I was talking about but it caught on . . .'

On 22 April, 2003, a closed-captioning typist for ABC's *World News Tonight* informed viewers that Federal Reserve chairman Alan Greenspan was 'in the hospital for an enlarged prostitute'. Later that evening, viewers were advised that Mr Greenspan was in fact having prostate problems.

In November 2009, British Prime Minister Gordon Brown hand-wrote a letter of condolence to a mother whose son had died in Afghanistan, during which he misspelled the deceased's surname. The *Sun* published a vitriolic article criticising his lack of care. In this article, the paper misspelled the same name and was forced to publish an apology of its own.

Arriving at Hirsch Coliseum March 5 are Sesame Street stars The Cunt, (clockwise from top left) Grover, Big Bird, Cookie Monster, Oscar the Grouch, Prairie Dawn, Ernie and Bert.

The greatest typo ever?

WINDOW OF JOHN FOWLES SAYS LANDMARK HOME HAS BECOME A DUMP

Daily Telegraph

He and his wife Gillian, who is a teacher, have three children, Gaven aged 13 and 11-year-old twins ugh and Helen.

Orpington News Shopper

MY FAVOURITE TYPO

Heather Brooke, Investigative Journalist and Author

'The following error appeared in the opening sentences of my book *The Revolution will be Digitised* – luckily only in the first proofs:

"As the cost of publishing and duplication has dropped to near zero a truly free press, and a truly informed pubic, becomes a reality."'

Eliot B Spalding, who was Editor of Massachusetts' *Cambridge Chronicle* for many years, recalls a misprint that, 'thanks be to God', he caught in proof. A caption under the front-page picture of a prominent society woman was supposed to read 'Heads monthly flower show', but the printer omitted two letters, making it 'Heads monthly flow show'.

The *New York Times* once committed a rather politically incorrect typo in an article about a man who had been abducted by Pakistan's intelligence agency, by misspelling the name of the Pakistani capital. They referred to it as 'Islambad'.

WHEN TYPESETTERS LOSE IT – NO. 147

Morgan met his accustomed pursuers, the newspapermen, when he emerged from the courthouse shortly before 1 o'clock. He varied his familiar phrase slightly by saying, hT" welawibej-fssufa-:cmfwypmfw.

Buffalo Courier-Express

A RESPECTABLE YOUNG PERSON WANTED, AGE ABOUT 81 OR 19, AS HOUSEMAID, AND TO WAIT AT TABLE

Advert in *The Times*, London, 13 February 1872

12 Aug 2003 – In our interview with Sir Jack Hayward, the chairman of Wolverhampton Wanderers, page 20, Sport, yesterday, we mistakenly attributed to him the following comment: 'Our team was the worst in the First Division and I'm sure it'll be the worst in the Premier League'. Sir Jack had just declined the offer of a hot drink. What he actually said was 'Our tea was the worst in the First Division and I'm sure it'll be the worst in the Premier League.' Profuse apologies.

Guardian Corrections and Clarifications

With its highly evolved social structure of tens of thousands of worker bees commanded by Queen Elizabeth, the honey bee genome could also improve the search for genes linked to social behaviour [. . .] Queen Elizabeth has 10 times the lifespan of workers and lays up to 2,000 eggs a day.

Reuters

NOTHING CHANGES . . .

'There will be slovenly reporters, and stupid compositors, and over-pressed subeditors, and careless or "sleepy" readers, to the end of time. One of the most marvellous facts in connection with the subject of newspaper blunders is the immense difference to the sense of a sentence which may depend upon one single letter, and, where the transformation effected by such simple means results in changing the original sense, not into mere utter nonsense, but into another sense, or into nonsense with a method in it. The result is a blunder often well worth recording. Sometimes, indeed, the results of a very simple substitution are so ingenious that it is hard to avoid a suspicion as to the purely accidental nature of its origins. When the unfortunate cow was described by a reporter as killed by a railway train, was it indeed mere chance, or sly humor, which substituted a *c* for an *h*, and cut the poor cow into "calves" instead of into "halves", in type? When the *Pall Mall Gazette* only the other day headed a political article "Mr Gladstone as a 'Force'", was it again simple accident which converted the *o* of force into an *a*, or was some enemy in the camp, some facetious Tory of the composing-room, to blame for it? . . . "Dudley's *house* was seen galloping furiously away with foaming sides," from a serial story in the *Natal Witness*, and "Mr Gibson carefully locked up his *horse*, which is a wooden and iron building" (*Natal Mercury*, Nov 12, 1883) may be said to cancel each other out; as may also the "importation of *deceased* animals", the heading of a paragraph in the *Daily Birmingham Gazette* some years ago, and "The *Diseased* Wife's Sister Bill".'

Frederic C. Williams,
Journalistic Jumbles:
Or, Trippings in Type, 1884

INTERLUDE

Punctuation Matters

A nineteenth-century New Orleans cotton-broker tele-graphed to New York to ask whether he should make any purchases at the quotations then ruling the market. The answer he received was 'No price too high'. He responded accordingly and bought as much as he could get his hands on. Only later did he discover, to his horror, that it should have been punctuated thus: **'No – price too high.'**

*

'Nude Reader's Wives' – heading in porn magazine. The intention is of course 'readers' nude wives'. As Lynne Truss points out, this conjures up the interesting picture of a polygamous nude reader 'attended by middle-aged women in housecoats and fluffy slippers'.

Parasol: a protection against the sun used by ladies made of cotton and whalebone.

from *The Book of Blunders*, 1871

INTERLUDE

MY FAVOURITE TYPO

Sue, The Bookbag

'The one that comes straight to mind was when I sent some flowers to a friend who had suffered a sequence of mishaps, any one of which would have floored most people. I telephoned the order and opted for a simple message indicating that she was in our thoughts. Unfortunately it emerged at the other end, minus an apostrophe, as **"Were thinking of you"**.'

17 Feb 2003 – In our piece about Frida Kahlo, pages 2 to 4, Friday Review, February 14, an unwanted comma replaced a necessary hyphen to produce the following, 'the legendary gangster, movie star and sensitive art collector Edward G Robinson . . .' We meant to call him a 'gangster-movie star'.

Guardian Corrections and Clarifications

PUPIL'S ENTRANCE
sign at a – presumably pretty selective – school.

INTERLUDE

In his 1818 *Principles of Punctuation*: or, the *Art of Pointing*, Cecil Hartley draws our attention to the difference a comma can make. He asks that we consider Luke 23:43, specifically the difference between 'Verily, I say unto thee, This day thou shalt be with me in paradise', and 'Verily, I say unto thee this day, Thou shalt be with me in paradise'. As Lynne Truss demonstrates, huge doctrinal differences hang on the position of the comma. In the first version, which is how protestants read it, the crucified thief 'skips over the whole unpleasant business of purgatory and goes straight to heaven with Our Lord'. The second 'promises paradise at some later date (to be confirmed, as it were), and leaves Purgatory nicely in the picture for the Catholics'.

MY FAVOURITE TYPO

Malcolm Edwards, head of Hachette Publishing, Australia

'I remember a sign in our warehouse estate, which should have said, "*Absolutely no parking. Offenders will be prosecuted.*" The only problem with this was that the full stop was missed out, and as a consequence, the impression was given that parking could take place with impunity; i.e., "*Absolutely no parking offenders will be prosecuted*"!'

3
The Word Stage
Typos of Historical & Political Significance

During the 1992 US presidential campaign, Vice President Dan Quayle visited a New Jersey primary school as part of a drive to promote George HW Bush's education policy, and inadvertently became a national laughing-stock in the process. Quayle agreed to help judge the school's annual spelling bee, but when one twelve-year-old student correctly spelled 'potato', Quayle had him return to the stage, insisting that he 'add one little bit at the end' and emphatically mouthing the letter 'e'. Quayle blamed the fiasco on a typo in the flashcard he'd been given by one of the teachers.

When General Douglas MacArthur was being touted as a presidential candidate in America after the Second World War, a banner in Japan read as follows:

WE PRAY FOR MACARTHUR'S ERECTION

As president, Mitt will work to expand and enhance access and opportunities for Americans to hunt, shoot and protect their families, homes and property, and he will fight the battle on all fronts to protect and promote the Second Amendment.

From Mitt Romney's campaign website, May 2012. Apparently he's so reluctant to limit gun control that he's happy for us to hunt and shoot our own loved ones.

MY FAVOURITE TYPO

John Davy, British Museum

'This isn't so much a typo as a premature printing, but I've always loved "Dewey defeats Truman", when the *Chicago Daily Tribune* prematurely announced the wrong candidate as winner of the 1948 US Presidential election.'

In 1924 Mr Rockwell compiled the genial orgy of the Rockwell family.

Boston Herald

There can be no scared cows.

Local government report (UK)

THE SOVIET GOVERNMENT HAS BEEN RECOGNISED BY GREAT BRITAIN AS THE AWFUL GOVERNMENT OF RUSSIA

Birmingham newspaper, 1924

THE SPEAKING COCK TURNS 75 YEARS OLD ON SUNDAY

The BBC's announcement of the
speaking clock's birthday, July 2011

In January 1971 a Bicentennial Commission in Washington, DC, sent out a newsletter referring to the approaching 200th anniversary of 'the Untied States'.

WHEN TYPESETTERS LOSE IT – NO. 472

Amidst a crowd shouting 'Down with shrdlcm-fwycmfwycmfwycmfwy m cshrdlshrdlcmfwy-shrdlushrdl mm traitors!' and general laughter, Trotsky's adherents were compelled to seek refuge.

Tokyo Advertiser

Some *Guardian* Corrections and Clarifications faves:

5 March 2001 – The Perils of Loyalty, page 22, Comment, March 1, we referred to 'the moral satin of Clinton's career'. That should have said 'the moral stain' etc.

26 October 2000 – In our obituary of Edward Goldstücker, page 24, yesterday, we said, 'He passionately opposed the distortion of truth and the fortification of history'. Falsification, that should have been. Our mistake.

26 Jan 2006 – In a conflict over the health service, the Tories accused Labour of 'shroud waving', not 'shroud weaving' (a column, page 21, yesterday).

 In May 2012, Mayor Naifeh of Edmond, Oklahoma, spent a day trudging from door to door delivering info-sheets about the dangers of under-age drinking. Delivered as part of a national event called Make A Difference Day, each of the 22,000 leaflets included a phone number to call in the event that a responsible Edmond citizen caught wind of an under-age drinking party and wanted to report it. Unfortunately for Mayor Naifeh, a typo in the phone number meant that callers were instead connected to a sex line promising 'exciting live talk'.

WHEN TYPESETTERS LOSE IT – NO. 851

As President Coolidge contemplated the state of the nation and the state of his own health today he was moved to joke with reporters . . .

'I've had a lot of raspberries before,' said the President with a smile, 'but these are the best I've ever had.'

Further, in explaining why he had postponed a local sightseeing trip he said: ffi ffi ffi ffi ffi ffi.

New York Herald Tribune

BREAKING NEWS: OBAMA BIN LADEN DEAD

Fox News

THIS IS AMERICA AND OUR ONLY LANAGUAGE IS ENGLISH

Anti-immigrant protest sign

ENGLISH IS OUR LANGUAGE —
NO EXCETIONS. LEARN IT.

Sign welcoming visitors to the
Village of Crestwood, Illinois,
from Mayor Chester Stranczek

2009 NATIONAL CONFERENENCE

Banner which appeared above a panel discussion
arranged by one-time Republican contender
Pat Buchanan about the merits of making
English America's only official language

 Some assorted Tea Party signs:

GET A BRAIN! MORANS

OBAMA HAS A CRISIS OF COMPETNCE

OBAMA! READ THE CONSITUTION!

RESPECT ARE COUNTRY:
SPEAK ENGLISH

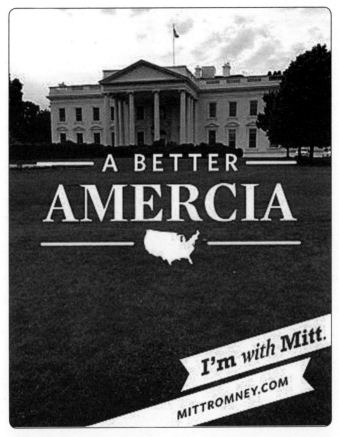

The ultimate gaffe? A photo of the White House taken with an iPhone and the 'With Mitt' app from the campaign of Republican Presidential hopeful Mitt Romney on 30 May 2012 in Washington, DC. The app allows users to take photographs with one of fourteen overlays including one that says 'A Better Amercia'. 'Mistakes happen,' Romney campaign spokeswoman Andrea Saul said on MSNBC. 'I don't think any voter cares about a typo at the end of the day,' she said, adding that an update had been sent to Apple.

INTERLUDE

The Typo that (Nearly) Deceived America

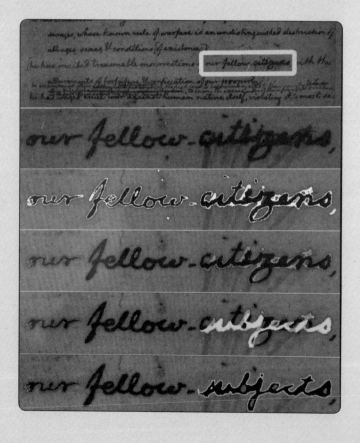

INTERLUDE

On 3 July 2010 the Library of Congress revealed some provocative new research on the Declaration of Independence. Using spectral photographic imagery, preservation researcher Dr Fenella France revealed that Thomas Jefferson originally referred to his fellow Americans not as citizens, but as subjects.

Jefferson is believed to have first written the word 'subjects' to describe the American population, and then replaced it with the term 'citizens', which appears throughout the historic document. Officials at the Library of Congress believe it to be a Freudian slip – even in the middle of declaring the United States' independence from Britain, it seems, Jefferson had not fully escaped the mindset of a monarchy. 'It shows the progress of his mind,' said James Billington, the US Librarian of Congress. 'This was a decisive moment.'

While many saw it as a Freudian slip, though, *Social Text Journal* were sceptical that this wording and rewording would qualify as a repressed idea percolating up from Jefferson's unconscious, and questioned whether such psychoanalytic parlance can be applied to a draft developed more than a hundred years before Freud came up with the concept. Instead, they argue that Jefferson was seriously wrangling with the implications of considering everyone a citizen, and struggling with the language of his time. 'The delicious image of the term "subject"', continue *Social Text Journal*, 'overlaid with the word "citizen" brought to mind American anarchist John Zerzan's critique of the post-structuralist parlance of "subjects" and "subjectivity". In his 1994 essay "The Catastrophe of Postmodernism", Zerzan lambastes the use of these terms as an abnegation of power, as a bowing of head and heart to a notion of governance ("governmentality") that refuses the radical

INTERLUDE

possibilities of autonomy. On this Fourth of July weekend, I find myself wondering broadly: where are we building spaces of autonomy, and where are we bowing like subjects?'

(Or he might, of course, have just made a mistake.)

4

The Lingua Franca

Typos Abroad

A French publisher once issued a manifesto dealing with several serious and important topics, titled *Les Coquilles* ('The Misprints'). The publisher was determined to have absolutely no mistakes whatsoever, and the most elaborate and arduous proof-reading precautions were taken. When it was finally printed he took one look at the title page and, realising that the 'q' had been left out of the title, fell stone dead. For while 'coquilles' means 'misprints', 'couilles' is used the way 'balls' is sometimes used in English, i.e. slang for 'testicles'.

The famous 'SOTP' sign, Dar es Salaam, Tanzania

WELCOME TO HOTEL COSY:
Where no one's stranger

India

Specialist in women and other diseases

Doctor's surgery, Italy

Teppanyaki – before your cooked right eyes

Japan

Roguefart

Cheese menu, French restaurant in Hong Kong

This crud is from the finest milk

Cheese menu, France

Complimentary glass of wine or bear

Drinks menu, Nepal

Our police: no refund, no exchange

Gift shop, Nice

To call a broad from France, first dial 00
Paris guidebook

Don't forget to sing in the box especified for the foreigner.
Mexican Immigration Form

Look out! Our new baby is on our car!
Baby on Board sticker, Hong Kong

The English philosopher Herbert Spencer (1820–1903) recounts a brilliant story about a typo in the closing sentence of a French novel. The author intended to end on a note of gentle yet sincere insight about the nature of the self, and the nature of love: *Bien connaître l'amour il faut sortir de soi* – 'to know love it is necessary to get out of oneself.' But the printers made it: *Bien connaître l'amour il faut sortir de soir* – 'to know love it is necessary to go out in the evening'.

You are on a tourist site. Please, take care for Rob.
French car park

Come Fartably Numb
Song title on pirated Pink Floyd CD, Hong Kong

**This area is entranse 2nd floor.
Don't shit down!**

Japanese car park

**Guests are requested to be as quiet as possible
in their rooms after 11pm so as not to disturb
the quest in the other room.**

Swedish hotel

At least it's fresh

You must be welly dressed on the road other-
wise you will be arrested and confiscated.

Guesthouse, Bali

Martini & nipples

Aperitif menu, Lake Garda hotel

Uncomplimentary pants

Label on boxer shorts, China hotel

French widow in every bedroom

Hotel advertisement

Please leave your values at the front desk.

Sign in Paris hotel elevator

Before entering this mosque:
Please remove your shoes.
Please remove your socks.
Please remove your hat.
Thank you for your co-ordination.

Istanbul

MY FAVOURITE TYPO

Ian MacBeth, Senior Bookseller, Waterstones

'A few years ago I went to see a very badly subtitled print of *La Dolce Vita* at the Glasgow Film Theatre. I have no Italian but my suspicions about the translation's accuracy were confirmed when, during the scene in which Emma finally confronts Marcello with his cruelty towards her, the line "Why don't you love me any more?" was rendered on-screen as "Why don't you love men any more?"'

Who is apologising here – the steps? The letters themselves?
(image © Mighty Red Pen http://wordpress.mightyredpen.com)

INTERLUDE

Tales of the Unexpected from the OED

Three riveting typo tales from the ultimate pedant's Bible, the *Oxford English Dictionary* (caution: not for the faint-hearted):

1) The proofs of the very first complete *OED*, published in 1928, were described by one who glimpsed them as, rather thrillingly, '**the most heavily corrected proofs ever known**'. One proofreader, the American Fitzedward Hall, apparently spent at least four hours a day, every day, for twenty years, examining and critically reading the proofs. He was a volunteer.

2) James Murray, the man behind the entire endeavour, very nearly included by mistake the word 'alliterates' *as a noun!!!* One of Murray's readers had come across the word in an essay by the American poet James Lowell. Murray could find no other citation, so wrote to Lowell asking just what the hell he was playing at; Lowell explained, in response, that it was clearly a misprint, ironically enough, for 'illiterates'.

INTERLUDE

3) One of the very, very few genuine typos to make it into the first edition of the *OED* was the word '**syllabus**', which isn't actually a word. It is in fact a misreading of *syllabos*, a term that occurred in early printed editions of Cicero that relied on an even earlier manuscript, in which the reading indicated as correct is *sittybas* (accussative plural of *sittyba*, from Greek *sittuba*, 'title slip' or 'label'). As Simon Winchester asserts in *The Meaning of Everything: The Story of the Oxford English Dictionary*, 'the word *syllabus* should by rights not be in the English language at all.'

5

Food for Thought

Gastronomic Typos

In February 2012, school officials from Methuen, Massachusetts, apologised for sending around 6,500 kids home with a lunch menu that listed chicken cooked, apparently, in the style of the Ku Klux Klan. Superintendent Judith Scannell claims the menu was supposed to list KK Chicken Tenders, with the KK standing for a creatively spelled 'Krispy, Krunchy', but an employee mistakenly hit the K key one too many times.

BENGAL CITY

Take Away Menu

BENGAL CITY
65 Great Titchfield Street
London WIP 7FL
Telephone: 020 7636 5618

10% Discocunt for Orders over £10.00

Eat, Ray, Love — Rachael Ray finds inspiration in cooking her family and her dog.

Front cover of *Tails* magazine, March 2011

MY FAVOURITE TYPO

Max Porter, Daunt Books, London

'After much searching in Sydney bookshops last year, I am the proud owner of a copy of the Penguin Australia *Pasta Bible* containing perhaps the most excruciating typo of modern times . . . It's pure wonder in situ. As typos go, I think it's got it all — a great big Rabelaisian *Curb-your-Enthusiasm* show-stopper of a typo; exquisitely awful.'

100 g prosciutto, diced

12 fresh sardine fillets

salt and freshly ground
    black people

¼ cup fresh flat-leaf parsley,
    roughly chopped

¼ cup red-wine vinegar

NOT TO BE TAKEN WHILE BEASTFEEDING
Warning on paracetamol bottle

Keeping all food under cover is the first step toward ridding the house of aunts.

Albany Journal

Best before Mar 10 9075

Packet of Hovis bread

Best before 30 February

Packet of Cripps Nubake traditional English muffins

For coping with unexpected guests, it is always a good plan to keep a few tons of sardines in the house.

Woman's Weekly

Chocolate potato cake: 6oz margarine, 1oz cocoa, 4oz mashed potato, 5oz self-raising flour, 433 eggs, size 3.

Woman's Weekly

Deep Fried Salt and Pepper Soft Shell Crap

Menu, Hurstville, Sydney

Lame kebab

Menu, Iran

INTERLUDE

Hubris

In a press release from a company that sells spellchecking software for websites, TextTrust proudly lists 'the 16 million we pages it has spellchecked over the past year'.

It does not help if the book is full if misprints and spelling mistakes.

Book review, *Spectator* magazine

*

22 Nov 2003 – Our apology (Corrections, page 27, November 19) for inacuracies, requires an apology. We meant inaccuracies.

Guardian Corrections and Clarifications

*

Preface to the second edition. The second edition is substantially the same as the first, except for a number of mispronts which have been corrected.

Seen in a book in Merton College Library, Oxford

INTERLUDE

According to a story that has gone around for over nine decades, a book printed at the Riverside Press contained extravagant praise for the company's 'poofreading'. Three well-known publishers – Edward Weeks, FN Doubleday and Ferris Greenslet – recalled the error in their memoirs, but each gave a different account of where it occurred.

THIS MANUAL HAS BEEN CAREFULLY TO REMOVE ANY ERRORS.

Erratum: In our last, for His Grace the Duchess of Dorset, read her Grace, the Duke of Dorset.

Dublin Journal

'There was a time,' writes Charles Bombaugh in his 1871 *Book of Blunders*, 'when correctness in print was held in higher estimation than it is at present'. He recalls the story of an experiment conducted by a famous Glaswegian printing firm, in which they determined that their latest work be printed without a single error: 'Every precaution was taken,' writes Bombaugh, 'to ensure typographical accuracy. Six experienced proofreaders were employed, who devoted many hours to each page, and when they had done

INTERLUDE

with it, it was posted up in the hall of the university, with a notice offering a reward of 50 pounds to any person who should discover an error. Each page was thus posted for two weeks before it went to press. The publishers congratulated themselves for having achieved the desired result, but when the book was issued several errors were detected, one of which was in the title page, and another in the first line of the opening chapter.'

By an unfortunate typographical error we were made to say on Tuesday that the departing Mr. — was a member of the defective branch of the police force. Of course this should have read: 'The detective branch of the police farce'.

New Zealand paper

*

THE SENATE OFFICE OF EDUCATION AND TRAIING.

Title of training directory for staffers on Capitol Hill, circulated early 2012. On p. 13 it advertised a course in copy-editing and proofreading.

6

Crime and Punishment

Legal Typos

On 13 October 1944, a North Carolina citizen was brought before a judge in traffic court for having parked his car immediately in front of a sign that read 'No Stoping'. Rather than pleading guilty, the defendant argued that the missing letter in the sign meant that he had not violated any law. Brandishing a Webster's dictionary, he noted that 'stoping' technically means 'extracting ore from a stope or, loosely, underground'.

'Your honour,' said the man, 'I am a law-abiding citizen, and I didn't extract any ore from the area of the sign.' The judge, after conceding that he hadn't in fact been doing any illegal mining, let him off, concluding: 'Since this is Friday the Thirteenth, anything can happen, so I'll turn you loose.'

 The *Irish Times* recently recounted a typo in a medical publication that almost made it to press, referring to '**John Smith, the rapist**', rather than 'John Smith, therapist'.

Do not sue Vicks Sinex for longer than 7 days without medical advice.

Packaging for Vicks Sinex spray

 In Wellesley, Massachusetts, a man once handed a bank teller a note that read: 'Give me your 10s and 20s and no die pack.' Distracted by the misspelling of 'die' for 'dye', the teller had to re-read the note several times to realise that this was an attempted stick-up. Indignant, she crumpled up the note and told the man, 'I'm not giving you any money. Now get the hell out of here.'

A notoriously loud-mouthed solicitor once wrote in a letter to a client that he would be going out shooting the following weekend, and would the client like to join him? On accepting, the solicitor wrote back enthusiastically: 'Excellent – let's hope we get some peasants!'

In 2005, police in Alnwick, Northumberland were furious to see that a fifteen-year-old youth was in breach of his ASBO, as he was arrested yet again for unruly, loutish, alcohol-fuelled behaviour. The authorities hoped magistrates would punish the youth for breaching his ASBO, but it transpired that, technically, he hadn't. Closer examination revealed that he had mistakenly been ordered not to be in public 'without' alcohol and that he was also duty-bound to act in 'a threatening manner likely to cause harassment, alarm and distress to others'. After the boy escaped punishment as a result of the misprint, the officials behind the mistake were asked to deliver a new ASBO with more appropriate wording.

James Mann, University Bookshop, Otago, New Zealand

'We recently had a recall from Thomson Reuters for *Brookers Public Law Legislation Handbook 2012* – it somehow made it into print with *Brookers Pubic Law Legislation* on the spine. Amazing how missing out one 'l' can make a world of difference.'

GETTING OFF SCOT-FREE, THANKS TO A TYPO

When Tennessee police obtained a search warrant for Joshua Hayes, they found bricks of marijuana, a safe full of cocaine, pills and cash, and enough weapons to arm a small town's police department. But when the intake judge was making copies of the multiple search warrants, he signed the warrant and wrote 10:35 *p.m.* when it was actually 10:35 *a.m.* The mistake was initially dismissed as a typo, one that had no bearing on the authenticity or quality of the evidence. Hayes was found guilty and sentenced to twenty-nine years in prison. But according to the Criminal Court of Appeals, any clerical error – no matter how small – invalidates the entire search warrant. Tennessee state law does not provide for an error on a search warrant, even if it was made in good faith, even if it's a typo. So all evidence was thrown out, and Hayes was let off.

A rather pompous solicitor once made a wonderful typo in his Instruction to Counsel, a formal document still written in the third person, and generally opening with a phrase such as 'INSTRUCTING SOLICITORS: Refer counsel to documents 12a, 14b and 27F . . .' On this occasion, however, the solicitor referred to himself instead as 'OBSTRUCTING SOLICITORS'.

Another solicitor was known for writing very long-winded, adjective-saturated and impeccably detailed Attendance Notes – the 'itemised bill' lawyers have to produce detailing exactly what they were doing during client time, and demonstrating the value of their notoriously costly services. Attendance Notes tend to be quite self-serving and exaggerated, so the solicitor in question was horrified to learn that instead of concluding his with 'extensively engaged throughout the entire day researching documents', he'd shot himself in the foot by writing 'expensively engaged throughout the day . . .'

'This mush is clear . . .'
Opening sentence by a judge reading from a legal decision by the National Labor Relations Board, 2009.

I will be the partner in charge of this matter and would be happy to act as your day-to-day contact. My fees are $700 per hour. However, due to the nature of the work involved, other members of the team will be assfisting me with a number of tasks and documents as and when required. They are charged out at different hourly rates and we will provide comprehensive details of these in our monthly invoices.
Engagement letter sent by senior partner in large US law firm to new client.

Phew.

**'I have really enjoyed my time here and it's
been a great pressure working with all of you.'**
Farewell email sent by departing lawyer to entire firm.

INTERLUDE

Break a Leg-End

Charles Bombaugh tells us that 'amusing results frequently follow the disjuncture of the letters of a word, and their transfer to the word preceding or succeeding.' He gives the example of a report of Lord Brougham's speech, in the course of which the distinguished orator referred pointedly to 'the masses', which the printer rendered '**them asses**'. Similarly, a firm in Cincinnati telegraphed to a correspondent in Cleveland as follows: 'Cranberries rising. Send immediately one hundred barrels *per* Simmons.' Mr Simmons was the agent of the Cincinnati house. The telegraph ran the last two words together, and shortly after, the firm were astonished to find delivered at their store a year's supply of persimmons.

This reminds us that certain words have to be very carefully typeset – not just the letters, but the breaks, as the following examples from Teresa Monachino's wonderful collection *Words Fail Me* show:

An inscribed book is one which has been signed by the author or some other person as a memento for the **not-able** recipient.

*

INTERLUDE

This internationally renowned, specialist bookstore carries an extensive collection of first editions that you will find **now-here** in any store in London.

*

Finally the bill would go to the House of Lords where we hope some of those **tit-led** gentlemen may defeat it.

*

Although some persistence is required by the children, their learning through **disco-very** often contributes more effectively to their education.

Dodgy breaks also give us the immortal statement from a student essay, 'Mary Antwinet is famous for saying "**let the meat cake**"', as well as the sign on a door in Sana'a, Yemen that reads **PHYSIO THE RAPIST**, and a reference to 'Andrew Lloyd Webber' **shit** musical' in the *Thames Vally Listings* newspaper. Finally, a headline from one of Britain's most popular daily papers:

One-legged model Heather Mills marries Beatles leg-end Paul McCartney

7

The Cost of a Comma

The Most Expensive Typos

The following typo appeared in Ottawa county's 2006 election ballot and cost the state over $40,000 to correct:

A proposal to amend the State Constitution to ban affirmative action programs that give preferential treatment to groups or individuals based on their race, gender, color, ethnicity or national origin for pubic employment, education or contracting purposes.

170,000 ballots had to be reprinted, said Ottawa County Clerk Daniel Krueger. The proposal in which the typo occurred was already controversial.

'My first thought was, "Oh crap,"' Krueger said.

$ In 1962, a typo by a NASA programmer resulted in Mariner 1 being sent into the ocean rather than its intended destination, Venus. The cause was a missed hyphen.

$ Early in 2010, Gregorio Iniguez, Managing Director of the Chilean Mint, was sacked after he authorised the production of 1.5 million 50-peso coins that spelled the country's name 'C-H-I-I-E'. By the time he was kicked out it was too late, and all 1.5 million coins remain in circulation to this day.

> **24 Aug 1998 – In a report on the Finance and Economics page, page 21, August 21, we referred to the £250,000 advance for Vikram Seth's prizewinning novel, *A Suitable Buy*. Although undoubtedly worth every penny, the book is actually called *A Suitable Boy*.**
>
> *Guardian* Corrections and Clarifications

THE $500,000 TYPO

Joe and Annemarie Curcio, from Tampa, Florida, thought they'd won $500,000 on a lottery ticket, but were told by the lottery company that the ticket had a typo – the winning number '1' was meant to be a '13' – and as such was not valid. Each scratchcard includes both numbers and letters for clarity; the crucial number 1 on the Curcios' card appears to have 'th' and the remnants of an 'n' underneath, suggesting that it should be 13, the result of a simple printing error. In response to the couple's fury at the idea that the company knew such errors occurred, a Florida Lottery spokesman explained that it has reportedly happened eighteen times before, but that they'd sold 12.3 billion tickets – giving a 'misprint rate' of just 0.00000000146%. The couple sued the state for fraud, resulting in a protracted legal battle lasting over five years, during which Joe passed away. Annemarie hopes she'll live long enough to see the money; the lawsuit on the case is still pending.

Swiss trader Kai Herbert couldn't believe his luck when his employer JP Morgan offered him the chance to relocate to South Africa, where his new salary would be 24 million rand ($3m). He subsequently discovered, after accepting the job, that the decimal point had been in the wrong place – it should have been 240,000 rand, a mere tenth of what he thought he was getting. Herbert tried to sue JP Morgan for the $3m, but lost in March 2012.

It is proposed to use this donation to purchase new wenches for our park as the present old ones are in a very dilapidated state.

Carrolton Chronicle, Ohio

Prudential – were here to help you.

Advert for insurance firm

Very nice hoe, out of town buyers considering.

Canadian Estate Agent listing

$ An order sent by telegraph from New York to a Philadelphia florist for 'two hand-bouquets' was made to read 'two hund. bouquets'. The astounded recipient of the box that followed refused to pay for 198 costly bouquets which he had neither ordered nor wanted. The florist sued him, and of course lost the suit; he then commenced proceedings against the telegraph company, and eventually recovered the amount of the entire claim.

Music swing chair £30. From 0 months to 1yr, baby bath plus poo £3. Baby dressing table + chair £5. Golf balls 20p each, 7 for £1.

Local newspaper classified

The Chicago investors put the land up for sale for $22 million in 2008, but got no takers. The Trust for Public Land made a deal with the group to buy it for close to $12, if it could come up with the money by this April.

New York Times

MY FAVOURITE TYPO

Ron Kowalski, estate agent with Ron & Susan Ass., Virginia

'When listing a home for sale, the proper spelling of descriptive words is imperative. One small typo can change the entire meaning of your message – and potentially cost you a lot of money. Here are some that I have come across in my 10+ years in the business:'

Fresh pain throughout

*

Heated poo in back yard

*

Custom inferior paint

*

Large walking closet

*

Ceiling fangs in all bedrooms

*

This homo is move-in ready

*

Huge dick in back for entertaining

*

Beautiful bitch cabinets

INTERLUDE

Inconvenient Truths

In his 1931 collection *Breaks: Humorous Misprints by Tired Newspaper Men and Others*, WW Scott begins by stating that 'in reading this little book . . . we shall see that, in additional to many a scandalous announcement, many a true word is also printed—by mistake.' Here, then, are a few typos that, ironically, are far more informative and accurate than what was originally intended.

All work cheaply and nearly done.
                    Ad for home decorators, *Perthshire Advertiser*

*

Erratum – in our last number, in speaking of General P—, the types made us call him a bottle-scarred veteran. The printer should have made it battle-scared.
As Charles Bombaugh writes: 'Unfortunately, this additional blunder was as expressively true as the first one, General P— being notoriously a coward as well as a drunk.'

*

INTERLUDE

Mr Winsor's other missive yesterday was an attempt to put the brakes on Notwork Rail, whose annual spending he wants down from £6bn to £4bn within five years.

Daily Telegraph

And finally, a cautionary reminder from those wizards of modern finance, bankers:

Save regularly in your bank. You'll never reget it.

8

Autocorrect Dytsopia

The Future of the Typo

So how was the date last night bro
Did you score
Not quite. First date we went to dinner and then walked her home
Then I killed her in the woods outside her house and left
Killing her seems a bit harsh. Did she order the lobster and filet mignon at dinner or something?
***************KISSED wtf

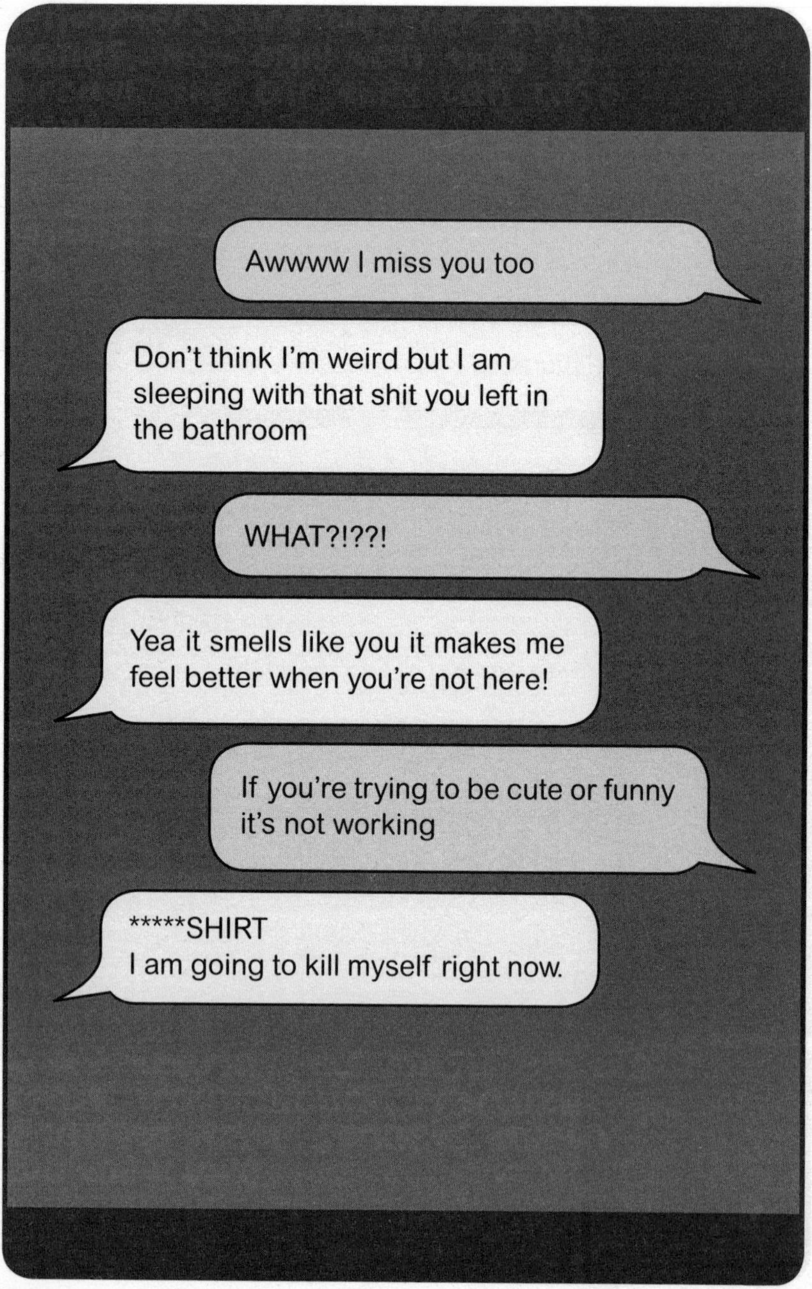
Awwww I miss you too
Don't think I'm weird but I am sleeping with that shit you left in the bathroom
WHAT?!??!
Yea it smells like you it makes me feel better when you're not here!
If you're trying to be cute or funny it's not working
*****SHIRT
I am going to kill myself right now.

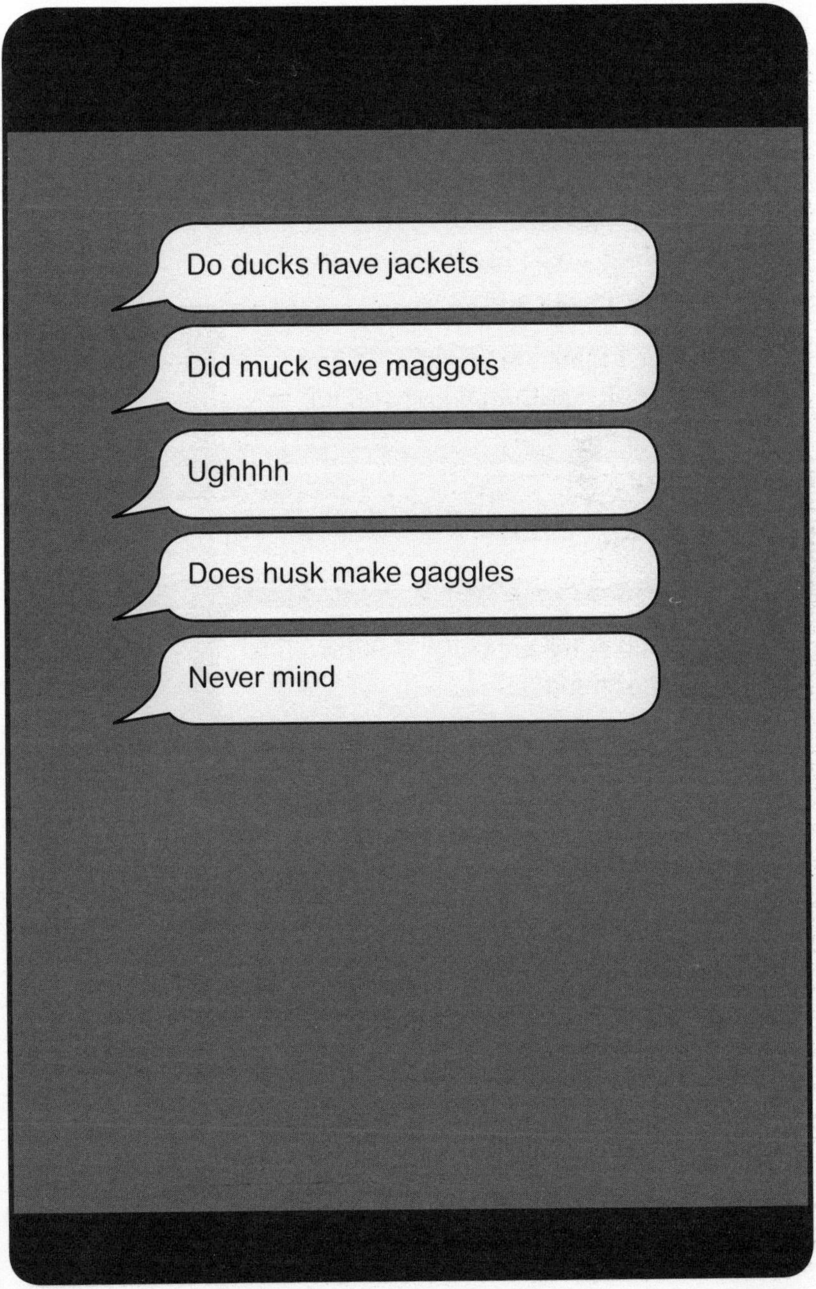
Do ducks have jackets
Did muck save maggots
Ughhhh
Does husk make gaggles
Never mind

On my way. Leaving the hairdresser's now.
Okay! How'd it go?
Great! I got a blow job at the last minute.
*Out! A blow OUT!!! Not the other thing.
I didn't know they offered that service. Haha

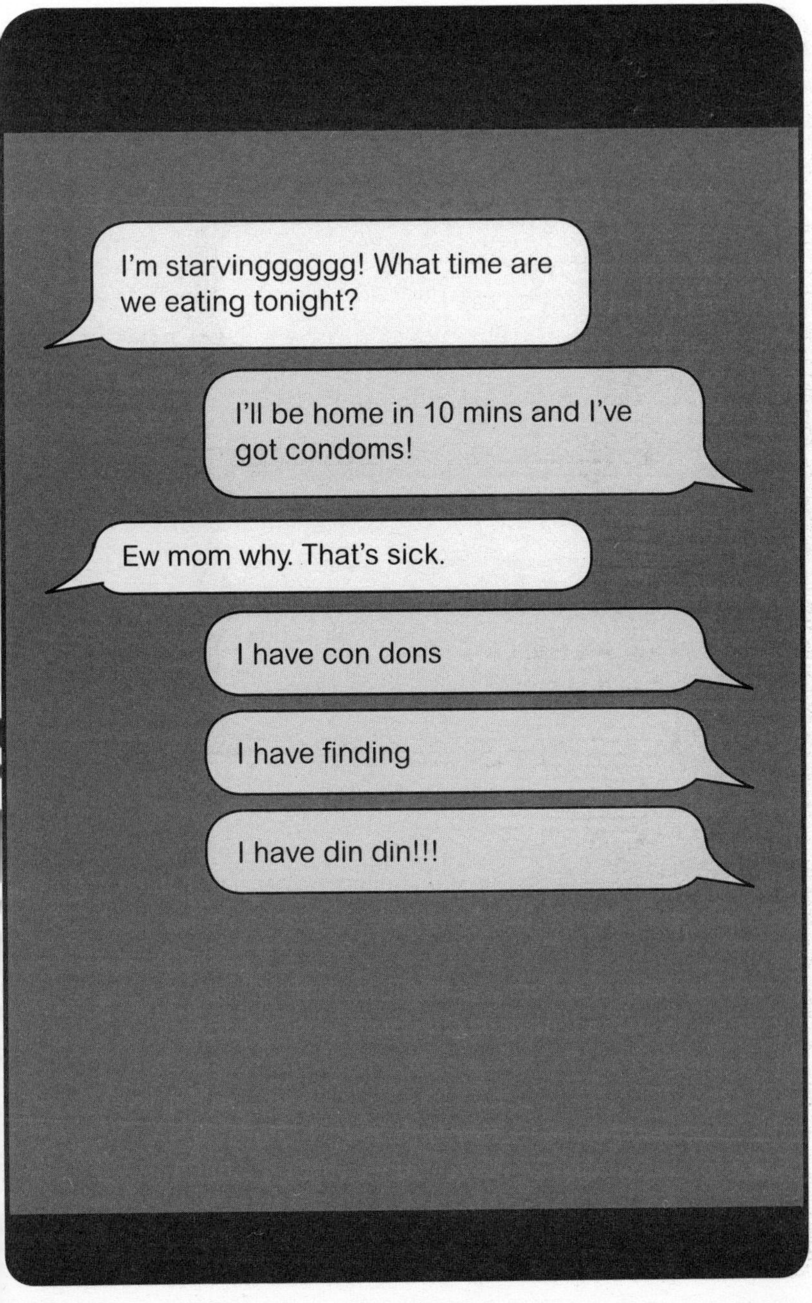
I'm starvingggggg! What time are we eating tonight?
I'll be home in 10 mins and I've got condoms!
Ew mom why. That's sick.
I have con dons
I have finding
I have din din!!!

Hi luvie . . . Saw ur pics on FB. Very cool. We are driving out to Montauk today so when u can, just call us on our cells ok? Cock
Oops xoxo
That was priceless.

Don't worry, seriously. He's crazy about you and he loves you so much. He told me the other day that you're the first girl he had ever thought about the führer with. Xx

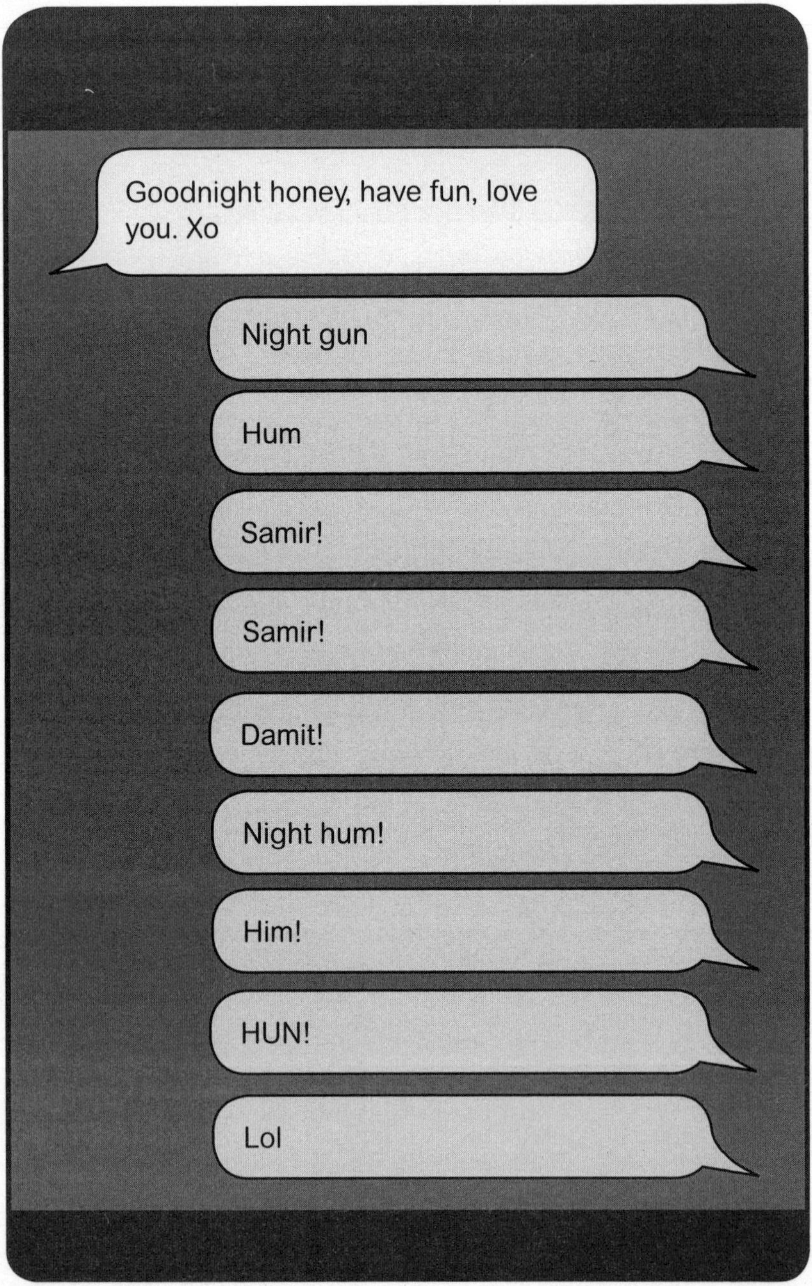
Goodnight honey, have fun, love you. Xo
Night gun
Hum
Samir!
Samir!
Damit!
Night hum!
Him!
HUN!
Lol

You have plans Friday?
No, why?
Do you wanna come with me to Rachael's going away party?
Sure! I'll orally come!

Will you be available for anal tonight? I'll be home in about half an hour.
Holy shit I wrote the word 'a call'
Not anal
Omfg . . . I swear I wrote the words 'a call'

Poop
Poop
Polonium
Ooooo
I think your phone just threw up on me.

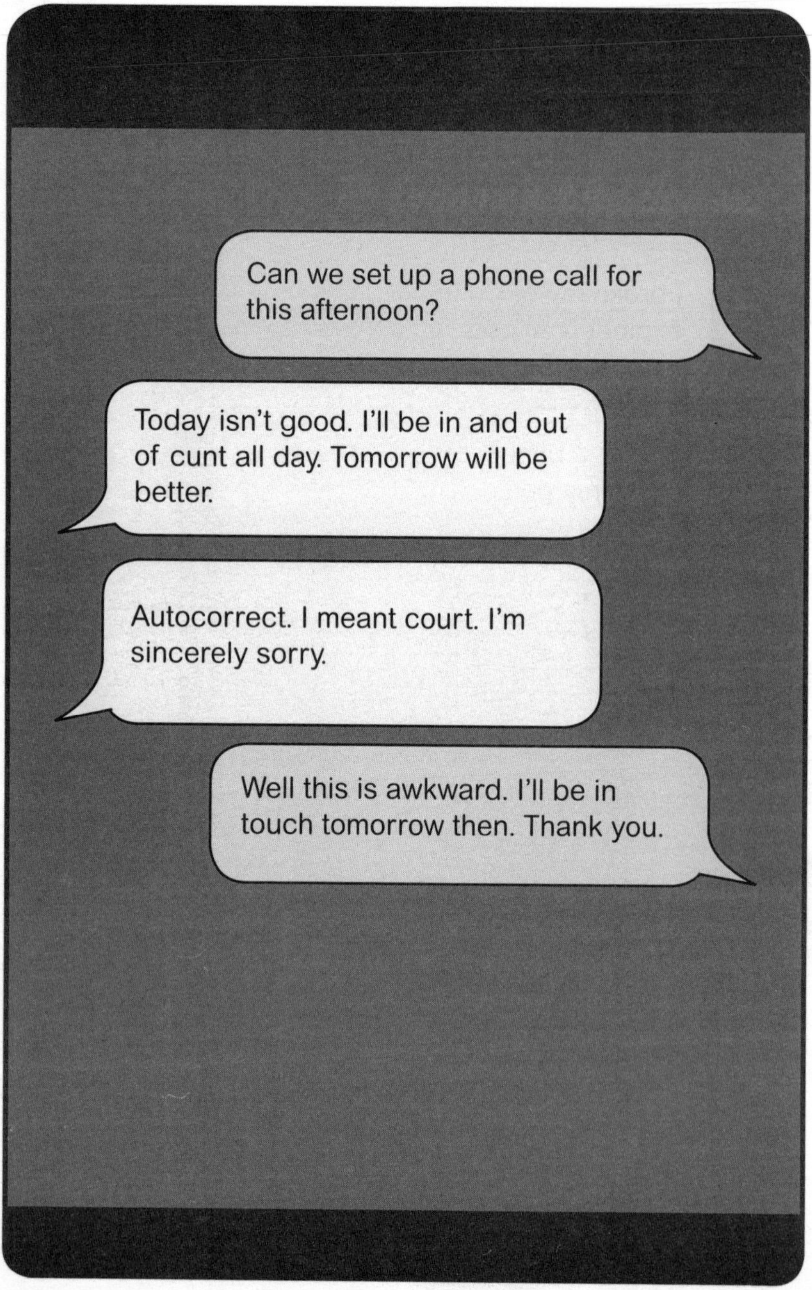
Can we set up a phone call for this afternoon?
Today isn't good. I'll be in and out of cunt all day. Tomorrow will be better.
Autocorrect. I meant court. I'm sincerely sorry.
Well this is awkward. I'll be in touch tomorrow then. Thank you.

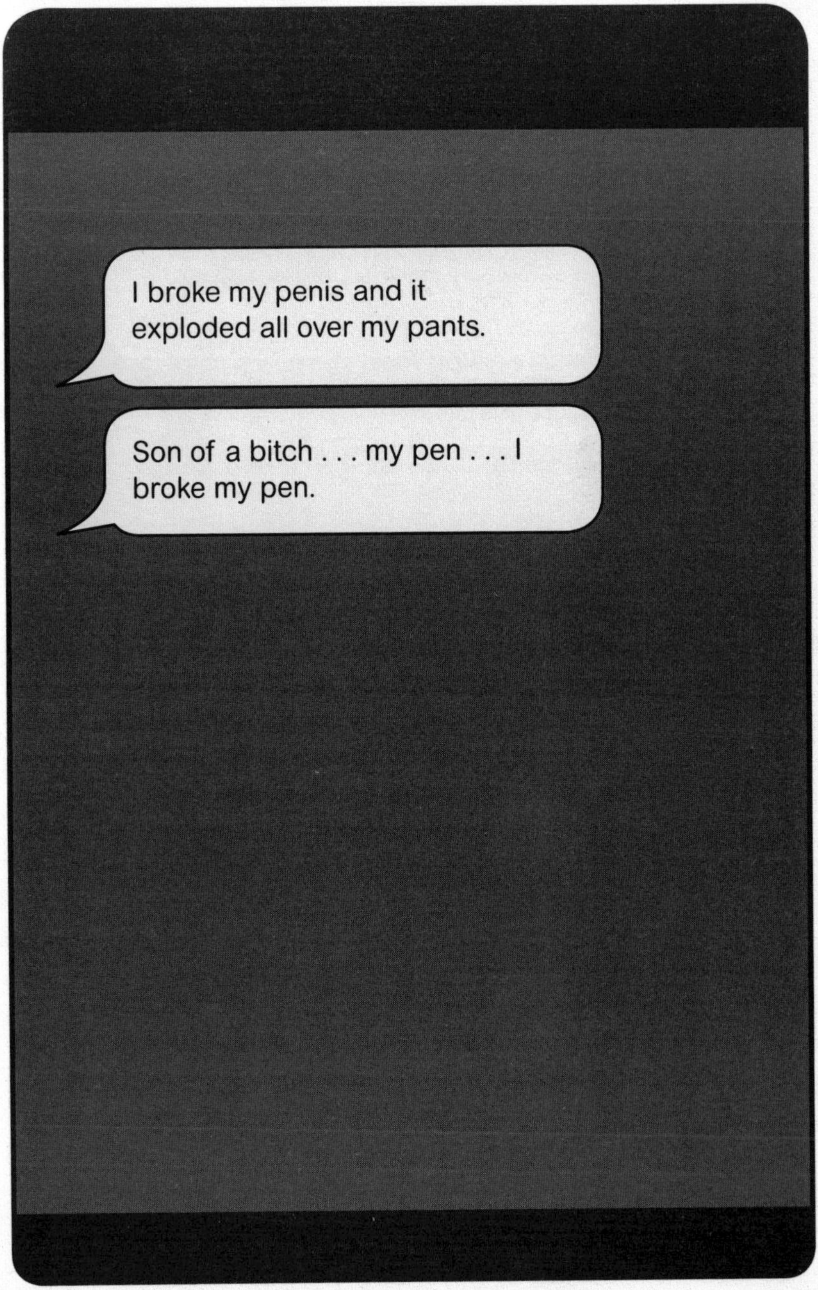
I broke my penis and it exploded all over my pants.
Son of a bitch . . . my pen . . . I broke my pen.

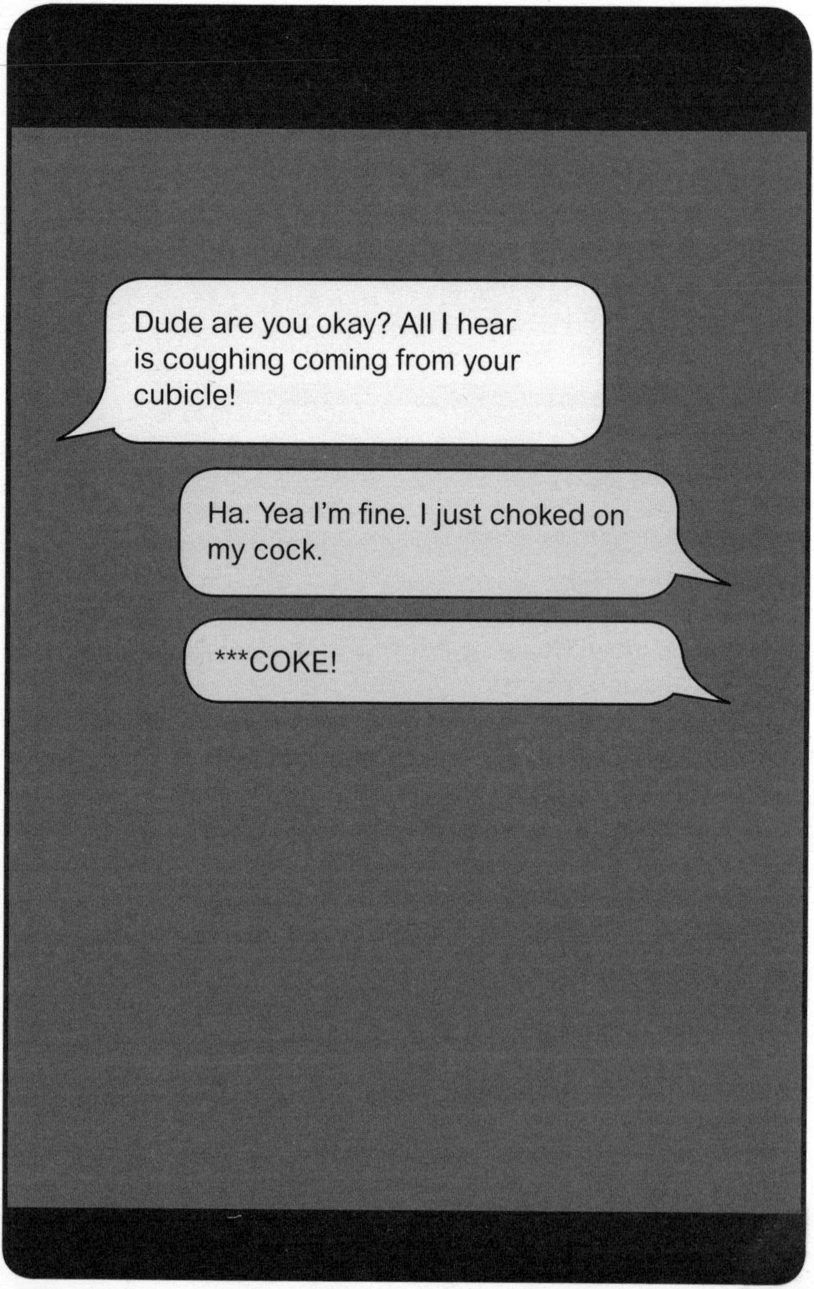
Dude are you okay? All I hear is coughing coming from your cubicle!
Ha. Yea I'm fine. I just choked on my cock.
***COKE!

How did the retreat go? I was so bored when I went last year.
Yeah it was pretty dull. Thank God Dave was there. He is hilarious.
I know! So funny. So you guys boned over the weekend eh?
Uh I'm not into dudes. That and my girlfriend would be pissed.
I meant bonded! Sorry, my bad. Autocorrect!

I can't find the jews to open the supply cabinet. Do you know where they are?
I don't know about the jews, but the keys are on my desk!

Don't worry if you get home and we're not here. I took the boys for a leisurely wank on the beach.
I'm calling the police now.

INTERLUDE

The Man Who Started it All . . .

A consolatory aside to those who beat themselves up about their woeful typing skills: the merchant William Caxton, who set up Britain's first printing press in Westminster in 1476, was both a path-breaker and a terrible typesetter, frequently asking his readers to 'correcte and amende where they shal fynde faulte.' Credit where it's due for sheer honesty: as Simon Garfield has pointed out, Caxton's 1480 *Vocabulary of French and English* is riddled with 'so many misprints that you feel like writing in disgust to the publisher'.

In Caxton's defence, there are some pretty tricky words in this text, and the majority of the typos were on the French rather than the English side, involving confusing particular letters (u and n; b and d etc.) – so 'eugaignies' instead of 'engaignies'; 'Descuriens' instead of 'Descurieus', 'coguoistre' for 'cognoistre', 'desiunerous' for 'desiunerons', and 'gausailliede' for 'gansailliede'.

INTERLUDE

Sadly none of the English typos are particularly funny, with the possible exception of 'byng of beme' for 'kyng of beme' (the lure of alliteration seems to have got the better of him), 'she' for 'he' in a clause also containing the phrase 'wrestling with a boy', and the rather glorious 'dooo' for 'dooe'.

9

Immaculate Contraption

Kids' Typos

In 2009, the *Times Higher Education Supplement* featured an article about examiners' favourite howlers. One biology student spent an entire paper telling Kevin Reiling, from the Faculty of Sciences at Staffordshire University, about the science of gnomes. 'It took me a while to realise she was referring to genomes,' Dr Reiling remarked. Similarly, a Dr Enticknap was told about a film being made undercover in order to 'draw attention to human rights abuses in the Best Wank and Gaza'.

'Sometimes,' comments the author of the article, Rebecca Atwood, these mistakes 'uncannily reflect the feelings of the examiner. When a finalist's commentary on a medieval French poem said that "all of the sentences end in a coma", Emma Cayley, Senior Lecturer in French at the University of Exeter, thought: "Yup, that's pretty much how I felt marking it, too."' Atwood offered many other examples:

A student at the University of Brunel told Gareth Dale, senior lecturer in politics and international relations, that the United States had the most powerful and advanced military in the world, possessing 'highly-developed and powerful marital equipment'.

Another misquoted Thomas Hobbes, explaining that the English philosopher believed 'people in the state of nature were nasty, brutish and short'. Hobbes was in fact referring to 'life', rather than 'people'.

Asked about the British electoral system in an exam, a first-year Politics student at Royal Holloway, University of London, told History Lecturer Rene Wolf about a system called 'first parcel post'.

Meanwhile, John Wilson, Placements Tutor at the University of Central Lancashire, was asked for a reference via the following message: 'Will you please be a referee for a job for which I am appalling?' The student in question wanted to be a teacher.

The reason students are so adept at making such laughable errors, of course, is that they have years of primary and secondary school to practise . . .

According to the Bible, Jesus was born because Mary had an immaculate contraption.

Rambo was a famous French poet.

Chaucer was the father of English pottery.

The theme of The Catcher in the Rye is that Holden Caulfield leaves the world of childhood and enters the world of adultery.

In India a man in one cask cannot marry a woman in another cask.

Q: How long is Lake Victoria?
A: Frifley big.

The Black Hole in Calcutta was a small dark prison
with ninety men and only one widow in it. In the
morning all the men were dead.

Another of the commandments is
'Though Shalt not kick a duckery.'

The Normans introduced the frugal
system.

You must always be careful if
you bite your lung. It may be
dangerous.

When Queen Elizabeth exposed herself before her
troops, they all shouted 'hurrah'. Then her navy went
and defeated the Spanish Armadillo.

One of the causes of the
Revolutionary war was the
English put tacks in their tea.

Abraham Lincoln became America's greatest Precedent . . . he said, 'In onion there is strength.'

The bowels are A, E, I, O, U, and sometimes W and Y.

After the snow-storm the dog found some tracts which excited his curiosity very much.

In spring the lambs can be seen gambling in the fields.

Blessed are the meek, for they shall irrigate the earth.

Unaware means the clothes we put on first.

Drake circumcised the world in a small ship.

'Hell hath no fury like a woman's corn.'

Wordsworth wrote an Ode on the Intimations of Immorality.

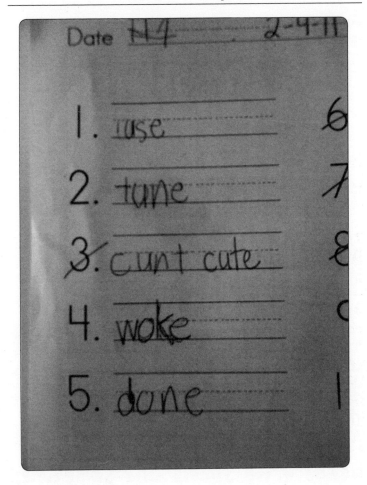

Date N4   2-4-11

1. ~~ruse~~   6

2. ~~tune~~   7

3. ~~cunt~~ cute   8

4. ~~woke~~   ~~C~~

5. ~~done~~   1

The first scene I would like to analize occurs in
Heart of Darkness.

A triangle which has an angle of 135 degrees is
called an obscene angle.

writing at the same time as
shakespeare was miguel
cervantes. He wrote Donkey Hote.

Finally, the colonists won the War and no longer had
to pay for taxis.

Queen Victoria was the longest queen. She sat
on a thorn for 63 years.

Dickens spent his youth in prison
because his father's celery was cut
off.

The scarlet Letter griped me
intensely.

This book belongs in the anals of English literature.

Defoe write simply and sometimes
crudly.

In the United States people are always put to death
by elocution.

Low wages paid by farmers were responsible for the Pheasants' Revolt.

The roe and the emu are prehistoric animals now extant.

You may be imprisoned if you use mallet and forethought.

What horrible deed did the Black Prince do at Limoges? He massaged all the people.

A noun should be declined and a verb should be congratulated.

Q: Use nitrates in a sentence
A: Night rates are cheaper than day rates.

Q:What are rabies and what would you do for them?
A: Rabies are Jewish priests. I would do nothing for them.

A ruminating animal is one that chews its cubs.

A census taker is a person who goes from house to house increasing the population.

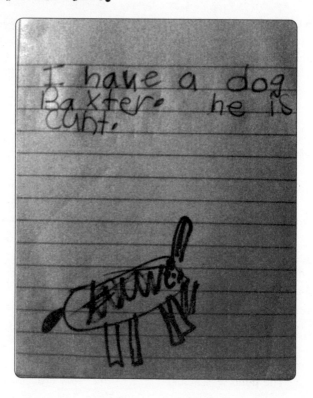

Joseph had a goat of many colours, but it got him out of the pit all right.

The pleasures of youth are very great, but they are not to be compared to the pleasures of adultery.

MY FAVOURITE TYPOS

Peter Ho Davies, novelist

'With apologies to my creative writing students, but with thanks too for their inadvertent poetry and subconscious cliché busting . . .'

It was like having a bitch you couldn't scratch.

*

The way she swung her hips it was clear she
was a wonton woman.

*

She cuddled up behind him, her arms encircling his waste.

*

The city had been obliterated by an unclear missile.

*

If you see him, do give him my retards.

*

The pond was stocked with plump, lazy crap.

*

The audience burst into thunderous apple sauce.

*

Oh, don't be mellow dramatic.

*

Helicopters are cleverer than planes. Not only can they fly through the air they can also hoover.

And there were rows of shelves in tears.

Doctors now treat their patients with ultra-violent rays.

Barristers are pieces of wood, generally at the side of stairs.

My brother is handsome, my sister is handmore, but my cousin is by far the handmost.

After Hitler got out of prison in 1924 he reorganized the Nazi party and came to a realization that in order for him to acquire power he had to work within the electrical system.

After hearing the music of the French troubadours, Petrarch began to write sonnets about courtney love.

A hostage is a lady who entertains visitors.

A polygon is a man who has many wives.

Emphasis in reading is putting more distress in one place than another.

In conclusion we may say that Shylock was greedy, malicious, and indeed, entirely viscous.

Coal is decayed vegetarians.

King Arthur lived in the age of Shivery.

Alexander the Great conquered Persia, Egypt and Japan. Sadly he died with no hairs.

Another Greek myth was Jason and the Golden Fleas.

The Turks manicured the pilgrims.

The King wore a scarlet robe trimmed with vermin.

In the middle of the 18th century, all the morons moved to Utah.

Hitler's instrumentality of terror was the Gespacho.

When things didn't go as planned, Stalin used the peasants as escape goats.

A mayor is a he horse.

In biology today, we digested a frog.

In the Middle Ages people lived in mud huts with rough mating on the floor.

The nineteenth century was when people stopped reproducing by hand and started reproducing by machine.

... and in case any kids are reading, a couple of reminders that grown-ups aren't perfect either:

Please excuse Pedro from being absent yesterday. He had ~~diahre dyrea direa the~~ the shits.

INTERLUDE

Typos on the Couch

'There are times,' writes Sigmund Freud in his 1901 *Psychopathology of Everyday Life*, 'when the most insignificant slip in writing can serve to express a dangerous secret meaning.' Freud and his followers spent a fair bit of time trying to explain typos, which, perhaps predictably, he tended to see as manifestations of some deep-seated, repressed issue on behalf of the culprit. My favourite example of his, involving nothing more than an upper-lower-case slip, was submitted to him by an anonymous correspondent:

'I ended a letter with the words: "*Herzlichste Grüsse an Ihre Frau Gemahlin and* **ihren** *Sohn*." ["Warmest greetings to your wife and her son" – in German the possessive adjective "*ihr*", spelt with a small i, means "**her**"; when spelt with a capital I, it means "**your**".] Just before I put the sheet in the envelope I noticed the error I had made in the first letter of "ihren" and corrected it. On the way home from my last visit to this married couple the lady who was with me had remarked that the son bore a striking resemblance to a family friend, and was in fact undoubtedly his child.'

Not so much a case in point, as a pointed case.

INTERLUDE

Similarly, Dr E Jones devotes an entire section of one 1911 paper to misprints. He recalls a young lady who was 'secretly engaged to a medical man whom we will call Arthur X'. She addressed a letter one day not to *Dr Arthur X*, but to *Dear Arthur X*, 'thus expressing,' asserts Jones, 'her desire to let all the world know of their relationship.'

AA Brill, another contemporary of Freud's, offers an excellent example of a Freudian typo. A patient wrote to Brill on the subject of his sufferings, which he blamed on anxiety about his financial affairs in the wake of a cotton slump: 'My trouble is all due to that damned frigid wave; there isn't any seed.' By wave he meant, of course, a trend in the money market – but what he actually wrote was not 'wave' but 'wife'. 'In the bottom of his heart,' states Brill, 'he cherished half-avowed reproaches against his wife on account of her sexual anaesthesia and childlessness, and he dimly realized, with right, that his life of enforced abstinence played a considerable part in the genesis of his symptoms.'

Dr Eduard Hitschmann tells the story of a doctor who repeatedly made an error in prescribing a particular drug. On three separate occasions, involving a single drug, he recommended a dose ten times the strength of what he intended. Luckily in each instance he realised the error in the nick of time, but what Freud found interesting was that the prescriptions were all for women of an 'advanced' age. With a bit of gentle prodding the patient revealed that he lived with his mother, an arrangement that had long inhibited his sexual freedom.

INTERLUDE

'We make slips of the pen more readily than slips of the tongue,' concludes Dr Freud. So we'll end with a genuinely spooky one from the man himself:

'An American living in Europe who had left his wife on bad terms felt that he could now effect a reconciliation with her, and asked her to come across the Atlantic and join him on a certain date. "It would be fine," he wrote, "if you could come on the *Mauretania* as I did." He did not however dare to send the sheet of paper which had this sentence on it. He preferred to write it out again. For he did not want her to notice how he had had to correct the name of the ship. He had first written "*Lusitania*". [. . .]Before the war his wife paid her first visit to Europe after the death of her only sister. If I am not mistaken, the *Mauretania* is the surviving sister-ship of the *Lusitania*, which was sunk in the war.'

10

Misprints of Biblical Proportions

Holy Typos

When people ask what I do and I tell them I'm an editor, they often look impressed, even jealous, saying that editing must be a glamorous, exciting job. I often respond by asking if they've ever proofread an index, or trawled through an entire manuscript cross-referencing superscript note indicators with the corresponding endnote numbers. They tend to have left by the time I get to the end of the sentence.[2]

But in the course of compiling this book I learned of a group of people even more diligent, meticulous, devoted and inspiringly pernickety than your average editor. For at Peachtree Editorial and Proofreading in Georgia, USA, only one book is checked for errors: the Bible. The company, founded by June Gunden and her husband Doug, 'exists for the sole purpose of ensuring accuracy in Bible publication.' Overawed, I contacted June to say how impressed I was to learn of their company, and she was kind enough to send me some examples of typos that have cropped up, through the centuries, in the Good Book:

- The 'Printer's Bible' of 1702 replaces 'princes' with 'printers' in the 199th psalm, thus rendering it **'Printers have persecuted me without cause'**.

---

2 Though just for the record, *nothing* comes close to the near-hallucinogenic thrill of spotting a typo in an index.

- An edition from 1562 has our Lord asserting, in Matthew 5:9, '**Blessed are the place-makers**'.

- The Barker and Lucas Bible of 1631 – also known as 'the Wicked Bible' – omits 'not' from the 7th commandment in Exodus 20:14, rendering it '**Thou shalt commit adultery**':

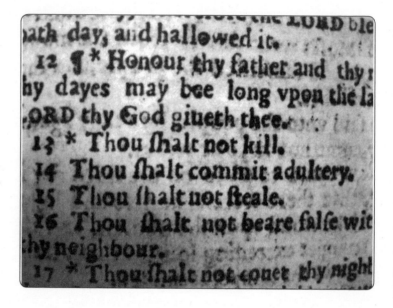

- The 'Unrighteous Bible' (1653) makes exactly the same sin of omission, asserting in I Corinthians 6:9: '**Know ye not that the unrighteous shall inherit the kingdom of God?**'

- In 1716, the 'Sin On' Bible implored its readers to '**Go and sin on more**' in John 8:11, rather than sinning *no* more.

- The 1795 'Murderers' Bible' reads, at Mark 7:27, '**Let the children first be killed**' (rather than 'filled').

Rejoice and be exceedingly clad!
Matthew 5:12 (from an edition printed in York in 1864)

The fool hath said in his heart there is a God
Psalm 14:1 ('not a God')

I will . . . that women adorn themselves in modern apparel
1 Timothy 2:9 ('modest'; from the rather hip 'Teenagers' Bible' of 1964)

He that hath ears to ear, let him hear.
Matthew 11:15 (from the 'Ears to Ear' Bible of 1810)

Simon Peter answered, 'Lord, who shall we go to? You have the message of eternal life, and we believe; we know that you ate the Holy One of God.'
John 6, 68–9

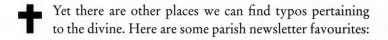 Yet there are other places we can find typos pertaining to the divine. Here are some parish newsletter favourites:

The choir will meet at the Larsen house for fun and sinning.

Smile at someone who is hard to love. Say, 'Hell' to someone who doesn't care much about you.

The widows of the church need washing badly. They are too dirty for any use and are a disgrace to our village.

YOUNG PEOPLE'S SOCIETY. Everyone is invited. Tea and Social Hour at 6:15. Mrs Smith will sin

To commemorate the Queen's Diamond Jubilee, Gunness Parish Council intend to place a commemorative plague on the village green.

As the ushers bring the offering forward, the congregation will rise and sin.

MY FAVOURITE TYPO

Chris Leftley, Librarian, Wycliffe Hall, Oxford University

'I have an erratum slip in the Library Office, which reads:

The publishers would like to apologise for and draw attention to an error that appeared in the third paragraph of the Foreword by Bob Horn. The paragraph included the wording "the personal involvement of God in *promoting* sin" which should have read "the personal involvement of God in *punishing* sin".'

Do not post pornography. Porn is bare female breasts and male or female gentiles.
General Forum Rule no.4 on gaming website PlanetSide.

The Bishop will then go to Chicago for a weep.
New York paper

✝ A New York theatre critic recalls 'a felicitous sin of omission' committed against his copy: 'by doing away with a final "t", they had me declaring, apropos of a revival of Mary Chase's comedy-fantasy *Harvey*, that the hero was accompanied everywhere by "an invisible six-foot-tall white rabbi".'

✝ In his 1860 tract *The Stillness of the Hour: or, Communion with God*, Austin Phelps wrote that 'the stillness of the hour is the stillness of a dead calm at sea'. Several hundred copies were printed and sold in which the word 'calm' was printed 'clam'.

MY FAVOURITE TYPO

Carol Austin, Copy-Editor

'As a copy-editor working on proofs of religious books, I used to see some unholy typesetting errors. Once at Christmas "Satan" became "Santa". And another time "God is self-creating" was rendered as "God is self-catering".'

It took many rabbits many years to write the Talmud.

Holland Evening Sentinel, Michigan

✝ Benjamin Franklin published a hilarious pseudonymous letter in 1729 about the perils of printing. He recalls:

'In a certain Edition of the Bible, the Printer had, where *David* says *I am fearfully and wonderfully made*, omitted the Letter 'e' in the last Word, so that it was, *I am fearfully and wonderfully mad*; which occasion'd an ignorant

Preacher, who took that Text, to harangue his Audience for half an hour on the Subject of *Spiritual Madness*.'

✝ Franklin goes on to cite an 'unlucky fault that went through a whole impression of Common Prayer Books'. The assertion that: 'We shall all be *changed* in a moment, in the twinkle of an eye', the printer had omitted the 'c', rendering it: 'We shall all be *hanged* . . .' The typo occurred in the Funeral Service pages, of all places.

MY FAVOURITE TYPO

Jenny Karat, publishing sales representative

'I did my publishing degree in the nineties and worked in the summer holiday at a small religious publisher in my home town. When photocopying a mail-out to go to customers (90% of which were Christian bookshops) I was idly reading through the jaw-droppingly dull press releases about the new books when I noticed that the heading for the Spring Titles had an extra 's' on the end of the second word in the heading.'

INTERLUDE

The Perils of Lifting!

In his 1884 book *Journalistic Jumbles*, Frederic Williams warns that there is 'a danger, pregnant with blunders, in correcting too much.' He continues:

'For, disturbance of the set type to correct one error sometimes brought about another. And, in "lifting out" lines of the type, as set in their metal frames or "galleys", for the elision or rearrangement of a sentence or word, it often happened that letters or words, or entire lines of type, slipped their places in the "galley", and got transposed in the line or in the column without the error being noticed until some atrocious blunder in the newspaper next morning revealed it to the horrified editorial eye.'

INTERLUDE

One example Williams gives occurred in an English paper. The words in italics were transposed: 'He was of *accidental* character . . . the jury returned a verdict of *excellent* death'. An even more 'atrocious mix' appeared in the *American Providence Daily Journal*. The offending article 'had reference to a testimonial to a departing clergyman; and another, descriptive of the erratic movements of a mad dog, got unfortunately engrafted upon it.' After referring to the clergyman and his sad state of health, the paragraph read:

So the congregation resolved upon a European trip for their beloved pastor, and on Saturday made him acquainted with the delightful fact. Accompanying the report of the committee was a nicely-filled purse, which was placed at the disposal of the pastor, who, after thanking them, made a turn down South Main Street as far as Planet, then up Planet to Benefit Street, where he was caught by some boys, who tied a pan to his tail. Away he went again, up Benefit Street, and down College, at the foot of which he was shot by a policeman.

INTERLUDE

My favourite by far occurred in a Montreal paper, and involved mixing an article on Catholic advances in Africa into a recipe for making tomato catsup:

The Roman Catholics claim to be making material advances in Africa, particularly in Algeria, where they have as many as 185,000 adherents and a Missionary Society for Central Africa. During the past three years they have obtained a firm footing in the interior of the continent, and have sent forth several missionaries into the equatorial regions. They are accustomed to begin their work by buying heathen children and educating them. The easiest and best way to prepare them is to first wipe them with a clean towel; then place them in dripping-pans and bake them till they are tender. Then you will have no difficulty in rubbing them through a sieve, and will save them by not being obliged to cut them in slices and cook for several hours.

11

The Best Love in the Whore World

Typos of a Romantic Persuasion

B ret Harte (1836–1902) once wrote in his California news-paper that a resident named Mrs Jones 'has long been noted for her charity'. The typesetter made it 'has long been noted for her chastity'. The proofreader put a question mark in the margin of the proofs, meaning that the typesetter should check the original copy. The article came out in the paper thus: 'Mrs Jones has long been noted for her chastity (?)'.

Arthur — was seriously burned Saturday after-noon when he came into contact with a high voltage wife.

Albuquerque paper

Words come easy to him – words that have a musical sway, words that come from an active mind, not marital words but those of peace.

Washington Post

Here the bridal couple stood, facing the floral setting, and exchanged cows.

Modesto News-Herald, California

Mr & Mrs Garth Robinson request the honor of your presents at the marriage of their daughter Holly to Mr James Stockman.

Wedding invitation

Acrimony, sometimes called Holy, is another name for marriage.

Child's homework

BIRTHS, DEATHS and MIRAGES

Smith's Weekly, Sydney

The bride was accompanied to the altar by tight bridesmaids.

Nineteenth-century court journal

WHEN TYPESETTERS LOSE IT – NO. 1,362

Charles Sales went to Kansas City Wednesday night to meet his wife his wife his wife his wife his wifezzzjdgwihwmyxETAOIN.

Buffalo Courier-Express

In the mid-nineteenth century, a certain Mr Jay preached a sermon before the Society for the Propagation of Christian Knowledge, and was asked to give his permission for the sermon to be printed. The text was from Job II:4: 'Skin for skin; yea, all that a man hath will he give for his life'. When the proof sheets of the sermon were sent to Mr Jay for approval, he found the text printed thus: 'Skin for skin; yea, all that a man hath will he give for his wife'. Instead of correcting the error in the usual way, he wrote in the margin, underlining the word wife, 'That depends on the circumstances'.

And they were married and lived happily even after.

Church World

**YOU ARE THE MOST AMAZING LOVE IN THE WHORE WORLD.
LOVE, JOE**

Message accompanying a dozen red roses, delivered to Joe's fiancée, from The Consumerist's *annual Valentine's Day 'Garden of Discontent'.*

Socrates died from an overdose of wedlock.

Child's homework

FALLING IN LOVE.
THANKS TO A TYPO . . .

In 2007, Rachel P Salazer lived in Bangkok, Thailand. Ruben P Salazar lived in Waco, Texas. Their email addresses were almost identical. One morning Ruben checked his email and saw that he'd received a note intended for someone else: 'It said "RP Salazar" followed by two numbers,' he recalls. 'I figured, "Hey, my email is the same exact thing without the numbers, so they probably sent it to the wrong person."'

Ruben, 39, noticed that this other RP Salazar was in Bangkok, so when he forwarded the email, he added his own little message. 'Something to the effect of "Hi, Rachel, it seems as if this message came to me instead of you. I'm in Waco, Texas, USA. Have a great day. P.S. How's the weather there in Bangkok?"'

This began a series of exchanges that would bring the two ever closer, despite being 8,000 miles apart. 'It's kind of like sending a letter in a bottle,' Ruben explained. He happened to hover his mouse over Rachel's name in an email, and her picture popped up. 'I was like, "Wow, she's really beautiful! How can I make this picture bigger?"'. Before long Ruben would be staying up late, when it was morning for Rachel, and the two would chat for four or five hours.

Eventually Rachel resolved to visit the US (Ruben told everyone he knew that she was coming; Rachel didn't tell a soul, as she realised people may think it rather barmy to 'go halfway across the world to meet some strange guy you have not met').

But Rachel arrived, spent the week with her cyber-totty, and on the evening of day six Ruben found himself proposing. They were married on 24 November 2007.

INTERLUDE

Don't Call Us, We'll Call You

Some CV howlers:

I have a graduate degree in unclear physics.

*

I am a rabid typist.

*

I worked for 6 years as an uninformed security guard.

*

As part of the city maintenance crew, I repaired bad roads and defective brides.

*

I have had sex jobs so far.

*

INTERLUDE

MY FAVOURITE TYPO

Kevin Dutton, psychologist

'I remember a colleague of mine at the University of Cambridge (who shall remain nameless) submitting a paper to a well-known peer-reviewed journal for publication. Previously he'd had a run-in with the editor of the journal, and for reasons better known to his analyst, had made reference in the text to a paper by "AB Fuckwit *et al*" while he worked on the rest of the piece. His intention, of course, was to tidy up the reference at a later stage once he'd checked the precise citation . . . but he forgot and, in a rush, sent the paper off unchanged. "AB Fuckwit" was, needless to say, the editor . . . who picked up on the clanger and rejected the paper outright.'

12

Life and Death

When Typos Kill

On 14 February 2012, politician Mojo Mathers of New Zealand's Green Party was proclaimed the country's first actively deceased MP, courtesy of a typo in a New Zealand First press release. Ms Mathers, who is deaf, made the news when a row broke out over whether her parliamentary note-taker should be funded from her own budget. NZ First reacted quickly to the news, speedily issuing a media statement announcing that the party would help meet the extra cost: 'This follows the refusal of the Speaker's Office to allow special funding for the equipment needed by Ms Mathers, who is New Zealand's first profoundly dead MP.'

OWEN. Phyllis. Six sad years today. Don't ask me if I miss you. No one knows the pain. It's lovely here without you dear, life has never been the same. God bless you dear.

Memorial in the *Bristol Evening Post*

Charles Bombaugh, author of the 1871 *Book of Blunders*, recalls that one biographer, in trying to say that the subject of his memoir was hardly able to bear the demise of his wife, was made by 'the inexorable printer' to say that he was barely able to 'wear the chemise of his wife'.

London, July 14 — Mrs Annie Besant, eighty-eight-years-old, was confined to bed today at the home of friends at Wimbledon. A severe child forced her to cancel all lecture engagements.

Houston Chronicle

Passengers must stay with their luggage at all times or they will be taken away and destroyed.

Sign at Paddington Station, London

Bea was preceded in death by her husband who died Oct. 11, 2007, one son, Mark Adrian Elston, her parents, grandson, Jeremy, and brother, Dale. She is survived by four sons: Verl George Jr. (Kathleen), Corin Lynn (Nadine), Ralph Wilbur (Barbara), and James Alan (Gena), one bother, Al, 16 grandchildren, 45 great-grandchildren, and two great-great grandchildren.

Salt Lake Tribune

On page eight, line seven, the words 'state zip code' should read – 'pull rip cord'.

A rather alarming press statement and correction slip issued by publishers Warrenton Fauquier of Virginia, for their 1977 *Easy Sky Diving Book*.

For 'died in infancy' read 'lived to a ripe old age at Orange'.

Corrigendum slip found in the *Australian Dictionary of National Biography*, 2001

Would you really, though?

☠ In her classic book *Eats, Shoots and Leaves*, Lynne Truss tells the story of the fatefully mispunctuated telegram that precipitated the Jameson Raid on the Transvaal in 1896. The Transvaal was a Boer Republic at the time. It was thought that the British and other settlers around Johannesburg (who were denied civil rights) would rise up if Jameson invaded. But unfortunately, when the settlers sent their telegraphic invitation to Jameson, it included a tragic ambiguity:

> **It is under these circumstances that we feel
> constrained to call upon you to come to our
> aid should a disturbance arise here the circum-
> stances are so extreme that we cannot but
> believe that you and the men under you will
> not fail to come to the rescue of the people
> who are so situated.**

If you put a full stop after 'aid', the meaning is 'come at once'. If you put it after 'here', it says 'things pretty hairy here, so we may need you at some point – stay tuned, we'll be in touch.' The message turned up at the *Times* with the stop after 'aid'. No one knows who put it there and, as Truss explains, 'poor old Jameson just sprang to the saddle, without anyone wanting or expecting him to.'

> **These Words were taken Notice of in the
> Article concerning Governor Belcher, 'After
> which his Excellency, with the Gentlemen
> trading to New England, died elegantly at
> Pontack's'. The Word *died* should doubtless
> have been *dined*, Pontack's being a noted
> Tavern and Eating-house in London for
> Gentlemen of Condition; but this Omission of
> the letter 'n' in that Word, gave us as much
> Entertainment as any Part of your Paper.**
>
> Benjamin Franklin's 1729 pseudonymous
> article 'Printers' Errors'

BIRTHS: On the 28th inst., to Mr and Mrs—, a bony daughter.

South African paper

'It's not far,' said Trevor. 'I'll soon run over you in my car.'

Short story

George had charge of the entertainment during the past year. His birth-provoking antics were always the life of the party and he will be greatly missed.

Willard Times, Ohio

Yoko Ono will talk about her husband John Lennon, who was killed in an interview with Barbara Walters.

TV magazine (US), 1987

WHEN TYPESETTERS LOSE IT
– NO. 2,111

Mrs Clyde —, of Pemberton, fell down stairs at her home this morning breaking her myhodududududududosy and suffered painful injuries.

Ohio paper

Mr and Mrs A. P. Hageman are rejoicing over the arrival of a mafwpycmfwpyemfwpycmfwppp doing nicely.

Youngstown Vindicator

In our obituary of Thomas Ferebee, page 22, yesterday, we said that President Truman had described the A-bomb as 'the *harmonising* of the basic power of the universe'. He said 'the *harnessing* of the basic power of the universe'.

Guardian Corrections and Clarifications

Police in Hawick yesterday called off a search for a 20-year-old man who is believed to have frowned.

Scotsman

A headline in an item in the Feb 5th edition of the *Enquirer-Bulletin* incorrectly stated 'Stolen Groceries'. It should have read: 'Homicide'.

Enquirer-Bulletin

The *North British Advertiser* of 22 April 1882 contained a tragic story of a young boy's death, who appears to have had a rather merciless carer. After describing the child's falling into a bath of hot water in his nurse's absence, the paper went on to say that the poor little boy was 'so fearfully scolded that he died almost immediately'.

The man blew out his brains after bidding his wife goodbye with a shotgun.

Connecticut paper

30 November 2000 – In our obituary of Conrad Voss Bark, whom we described as a journalist and fly-fishing enthusiast, page 24, yesterday, we said his pastimes included typing files. He much preferred tying flies, of course. The obituarist is exonerated.

Guardian Corrections and Clarifications

Last month, the Centers for Disease Control released new figures charting the HIV epidemic among black, gay men in D.C. The figures are grim: One in three black men who have sex with me in the District is HIV-positive.

Washington-centric news website TBD,
October 2008

FINALE 1

Muphry's Law

Muphry's law is an adage that states that 'if you write anything criticising editing or proofreading there will be a fault of some kind in what you have written'.

John Bangsund of the Society of Editors in Victoria, Australia identified Muphry's law as 'the editorial application of the better-known Murphy's law' and set it down in 1992 in the Society of Editors Newsletter.

The law, as set out by Bangsund, states that:

(a) if you write anything criticising editing or proofreading, there will be a fault of some kind in what you have written;

(b) if an author thanks you in a book for your editing or proofreading, there will be mistakes in the book;

(c) the stronger the sentiment expressed in (a) and (b), the greater the fault;

(d) any book devoted to editing or style will be internally inconsistent.

Muphry's Law also dictates that, if a mistake is as plain as the nose on your face, everyone can see it but you. Your readers will always notice errors in a title, in headings, in the first paragraph of anything, and in the top lines of a new page. These are the very places where authors, editors and proofreaders are most likely to make mistakes.

FINALE 2

(not really a typo, but hey)

Associated Press

Jodee Berry of Panama City, Fla., sits with her toy Yoda at her lawyer's office Wednesday. Berry, a former Hooters waitress, has sued the restaurant where she worked saying she was promised a new Toyota for winning a beer sales contest in April. Berry, 26, believed that she had won a new car, but she was blindfolded, led to the parking lot and presented a toy Yoda, the little green guy from Star Wars.

Acknowledgements

Without numerous generous contributions from book-sellers, journalists, librarians, authors, literary editors, copy-editors, proofreaders, lawyers and publishers, this book would have been even shorter. So a huge thank you to all those loyal typo-spotters who wrote, called or just turned up in my office with examples, and of course everyone who helped solicit contributions. Some of you asked to remain anonymous, for obvious reasons, but sincerest thanks to the rest of you, including: Erica Wagner, Alan Titchmarsh, Andrew Steeds, Nigel Wilcockson, Simon Heffer, Heather Brooke, Boyd Tonkin, Alastair Campbell, Sue Magee, John Davy, Sofia Romero of the wonderful blog Mighty Red Pen, Mary Dalmau, Max Porter, Judith Flanders, James Mann, Dan Franklin, Ben Johncock, Catriona McPherson, Jim Moir, Justine Taylor, Sarah Emsley, Suzie Dooré, Ron Kowalski, Ian MacBeth, Ed Faulkner, June Gunden, Dani Johnson, Carol Austin, Peter Ho Davies, Chris Leftley, Jenny Karat, Gillian Mackay, Kevin Dutton, Rose Alexander, Malcolm Edwards, Robert Watkins, Danielle Johnson, Sharon Huerta, Tristan Gooley and William Rycroft.

The truly bookish among you will have noticed that this is not the first collection to celebrate the art of the typographical cock-up.[3] Accordingly, some of the richest sources for the

---

3 Though those among you who possess truly Jedi-like powers of literary geek-iness *will* know that *Just My Typo* is the first book to concentrate almost entirely on a single letter, punctuation mark or space being in the wrong place at the wrong time. If you missed this, congratulate yourself on at least reading this footnote – I salute you.

funniest examples have been the oldest ones. Charles Bombaugh's *The Book of Blunders* (1871), Frederic C Williams' *Journalistic Jumbles: Or, Trippings in Type* (1884) and Benjamin Franklin's pseudonymous letter 'Printers' Errors' (1729) provided some wonderful pre-twentieth-century examples.

WW Scott's *Breaks: Unintentional Errors by Tired Newspapermen and Others* (1931) was inspiring for both its content and its impeccable subtitle. Highgate schoolmaster Cecil Hunt published various books of children's errors, and many of the examples from Chapter 9 are taken from his *My Favourite Howlers* (1951). Richard Lederer's *Anguished English* (1987) and Max Hall's *An Embarrassment of Misprints* (1995) offered some excellent American examples.

Freud's *The Psychopathology of Everyday Life* (1901, trans. 1960) provided all of the stories found in the 'typos on the couch' interlude. The *OED* interlude owes much to Simon Winchester's *The Meaning of Everything* (2003), and the punctuation interlude to Lynne Truss's now classic *Eats, Shoots and Leaves* (2005). Ian Mayes' *Only Correct* (2005) contains the very best of the *Guardian*'s Corrections and Clarifications column, and Charlie Croker's two wonderful collections of linguistic mishaps abroad, *Lost in Translation* (2006) and *Still Lost in Translation* (2007), were indispensable for Chapter 4. Norman McGreevy's *Must Try Harder* (2006) supplemented Rebecca Atwood's excellent *THES* article of August 2009 and Cecil Hunt's aforementioned work for educational typos, and Jillian Madison's *Damn You Autocorrect!* (2011) was invaluable for Chapter 8. The late Peter Haining's *Wrotten English* (2011, originally *Slips of the Pen*) is a superb and immaculate collection of literary trivia and embarrassments, and Martin Toseland's devastatingly funny and comprehensive *A Steroid Hit the Earth* (2008) was equally valuable.

Teresa Monachino's brilliant and highly recommended collection *Words Fail Me* introduced me to both dodgy word breaks and oxycretins. Patrick Forsyth's *Empty When Half Full* (2011) is a hilarious paean to the absurdities of marketing language. Lastly, Simon Garfield's *Just My Type* (2010) inspired both the nerdiness to read Caxton's 1480 *Vocabulary of French and English* and, of course, the title. Thanks also to the Library of Congress librarian who replied to my request with the following message: 'Alas, we tried. The Library's Public Affairs Office advises that we would only be able to send typos that are funny without being dirty or offensive. We were also advised to not send our own typos or those of the United States Congress. What was left, well, just wasn't very funny. Except one, which we find on the Internet from time to time: "Untied Nations", where the intent was clearly, "United Nations". Good luck with your book.'

Huge thanks go to everyone at Sceptre and Hodder for their general peerlessness and brilliance. The marketing team have been the most prolific by far in terms of email contributions (a nice rabbity typo, 'hop you had a pleasant Easter'; 'it would be great to get an update on thongs'; 'can I ask him to shit the money from May into July?' – if only the finance bods could produce money so easily). Thanks in particular to Bea Long, Rosie Gailer, Ben Summers, Angie Willocks, Juliet Brightmore, Craig Burgess, Tara Gladden for her incisive copyediting, Jonathan Price, Dave Cradduck for his superb index, the brilliant Kate Miles and of course to Rupert Lancaster, *il miglior editore*, for his expertise and enthusiasm from the very start.

In the course of compiling *Just My Typo*, my fiancée was promoted to wife, and endured many, many hours of not-always-that-interesting-or-amusing stories about typos, which she bore with Job-like patience. The experience clearly affected her (she managed to state that we were getting 'marrieid' on the wedding invitation she embroidered), but she has been characteristically wonderful about the entire thing. Thank you, Frances, for being perfect, even if Im not.

Index

Join a literary community of
like-minded readers who seek out
the best in contemporary writing.

From the thousands of submissions Sceptre
receives each year, our editors select the books
we consider to be outstanding.

We look for distinctive voices, thought-provoking
themes, original ideas, absorbing narratives and
writing of prize-winning quality.

If you want to be the first to hear about our
new discoveries, and would like the chance to
receive advance reading copies of our books
before they are published, visit

www.sceptrebooks.co.uk

Follow @sceptrebooks

'Like' SceptreBooks

Watch SceptreBooks

What Did We Miss?

If you have a favourite funny typo, send it to us at
justmytypo@hodder.co.uk.

The best ones will be included in future editions.